"The only thing of interest to me as a theologian of the church when it comes to politics is something that dissects and decimates the current Christian alliances with American political parties. Someone once said the mainline church lost its grip among American mainline Christians because it was no longer distinguishable from *The New York Times*, and someone now needs to warn conservative evangelicals that it is losing its grip on its people because it is no longer distinguishable from Fox News. If you would like an alternative, read this tart, sassy, and, yes, strategic book that presses us to see the church as a politic. Agree or not, he's an equal opportunity critic."

— SCOT MCKNIGHT
author of *The Jesus Creed*

"In this well-written and concisely argued work, Lee Camp masterfully traces how the church in America has to a large degree lost its all-important 'scandalous witness' while suggesting ways we can begin to recover it. In the process, Camp provides us with a remarkably clear, carefully nuanced, and undeniably compelling defense of a biblical understanding of the kingdom of God. He brilliantly exposes just how wide the gap is between the biblical understanding of the kingdom, on the one hand, and what currently passes as the Christian faith in America, on the other."

— GREG BOYD
author of *The Myth of a Christian Nation*

"With his emancipated evangelical witness, Lee Camp boldly exposits the reality of a gospel faith that is deeply political. This book issues a compelling invitation of gospel hope as the engine for generative public engagement. This is a welcome book, one that is sure to evoke fresh thinking and fresh action."

— WALTER BRUEGGEMANN
Columbia Theological Seminary

"Bold, urgent, uncompromising, courageous, and prophetic. Every page of *Scandalous Witness* surprises, shocks, and subverts. And all of it is absolutely necessary. American Christianity has lost its way, and Lee Camp has written the political manifesto the church needs 'for such a time as this.'"

— RICHARD BECK
author of *Stranger God* and *Trains, Jesus, and Murder: The Gospel According to Johnny Cash*

"Lee Camp's *Scandalous Witness* is balm for the politically weary Christian's soul. In a series of astringent commentaries, Camp impales pretty much every Christian sacred cow, whether right or left politically. Operating from a robust eschatological-ecclesial vision, Camp diagnoses much of what has gone wrong with US Christian politics from within his disciplined theological outlook and offers a contrarian statement that is up to the minute in its relevance. I highly recommend this brief and extremely helpful book."

— DAVID GUSHEE
Mercer University, past president of
the American Academy of Religion

"With a scholar's eye and a storyteller's knack for narrative, Lee Camp exposes the current inability of American Christianity to bear witness to the gospel. We are asking the wrong questions, taking the wrong turns, and pledging the wrong loyalties. Both parts contrarian and constructionist, Camp finds himself in the family tree of St. Paul, Augustine, Hauerwas, Davison Hunter, and others, challenging those who call themselves Christians to rearrange our bastardized version of the faith toward a more prophetic, historical, and theologically courageous imagination."

— DREW HOLCOMB
Magnolia Records recording artist

SCANDALOUS WITNESS

*A Little Political Manifesto
for Christians*

Lee C. Camp

WILLIAM B. EERDMANS PUBLISHING COMPANY
GRAND RAPIDS, MICHIGAN

Wm. B. Eerdmans Publishing Co.
4035 Park East Court SE, Grand Rapids, Michigan 49546
www.eerdmans.com

26 25 24 23 22 21 20   1 2 3 4 5 6 7

ISBN 978-0-8028-7735-2

Library of Congress Cataloging-in-Publication Data

A catalog record for this book is available from the Library of Congress.

Contents

CONTENTS

Acknowledgments

I dedicate this book to my colleagues at Lipscomb University, a delightful community, which has given me the privilege to teach and play and work and lecture and write and produce, and also to argue and laugh and complain and care about things that matter, and also to know the beauty of old and long friendships. I never anticipated how much joy and adventure an academic community might afford, and I shall always be grateful. Of course I do not presuppose that all my colleagues will agree with the arguments herein. This fact but reminds me again that we are a community that knows how to have worthwhile and good arguments, all while sharing a common love and vocation and tender-kindness one for the other.

For helpful feedback on this project, I would especially like to thank the MDiv Cohort of Hazelip School of Theology (class of 2019), my MDiv Christian Ethics course (fall 2019), and two different Sunday school classes at Otter Creek church. All of these groups honored me by allowing me to work through versions of this material, and they provided immensely helpful feedback. A colloquy of my faculty colleagues also read a version of the manuscript and similarly provided generous feedback. I especially thank Josh Strahan, Lauren White, Phillip Camp, Earl Lavender, Frank Guertin, Terry Briley, Mark Black, Richard Hughes, Walter Surdacki, Jim Arnett, Robert Chandler, Steve Sabin, Adam Boggess, and Stan Wilson. I am grateful for both the leave time and the support generously granted by Provost Craig Bledsoe and Dean Leonard Allen to work on this project. I especially thank Trevor Thompson in his vision to bring this work to press, along with the staff at Eerdmans for making the publication possible.

Finally, I give thanks for my lovely wife Laura, who has continued to live and labor and laugh and love alongside me all these many years now, and my dear sons Chandler, David, and Ben.

Introduction

A revolution is supposed to be a change that turns everything completely around. But the ideology of political revolution will never change anything except appearances. There will be violence, and power will pass from one party to another, but when the smoke clears and the bodies of all the dead men are underground, the situation will be essentially the same as it was before: there will be a minority of strong men in power exploiting all the others for their own ends. There will be the same greed and cruelty and lust and ambition and avarice and hypocrisy as before.

For the revolutions of men change nothing. The only influence that can really upset the injustice and iniquity of men is the power that breathes in Christian tradition.

THOMAS MERTON

The faith of the Christian is the last great hope of earth.

This must be the case if its most basic claims be true. Christianity claims, at its most basic, that captivity has been taken captive and death has been overcome. More, the fundamental claim of God as three-in-one maintains that it is through the gracious initiative of God's redemption, the suffering love of Christ, and the resurrecting power of the Spirit that the triumph of life over death has begun. We live now in a time of hopeful anticipation of the consummate triumph of life over death.

We must imagine Christianity first and foremost not as a religion but as an interpretation of human history or, perhaps more pointedly, an assertion regarding human history. But it is not and must not be understood simply as an intellectual interpretation of history but as the sort of interpretation that requires a particular way of life.

In other words, it is an interpretation, a claim about history that is inherently political.

Perhaps in all historical epochs there is a sense of crisis. This is certainly true in our own day. A mere seventy years ago, humans were first faced with the possibility of our own global destruction by technologies of our own making. This threat has grown ever more palpable, the technical means for such destruction multiplied, and new threats ever on the horizon. Today we do not face merely nuclear holocaust but the very undoing of the ecosystem, the destruction of all traditional forms of community, and the potential loss of the very meaning of being human with the rise of artificial intelligence and transhumanism. Our affluence in the West is correlated with a state of constant war, escalating rates of suicide among the young, and an increasing chasm between rich and poor.

Meanwhile, large portions of the Christian church in America appear to have destroyed their own witness, lacking the ability to speak truthfully or prophetically or carefully. The recent commentary by the conservative political commentator Andrew Sullivan provides a glimpse of the public joke that American Christianity has become. Critiquing the Right, he says,

> Yes, many Evangelicals are among the holiest and most quietly devoted people out there. Some have bravely resisted the cult. But their leaders have tribalized a religion explicitly built by Jesus as anti-tribal. They have turned to idols—including their blasphemous belief in America as God's chosen country. They have embraced wealth and nationalism as core goods, two ideas utterly anathema to Christ. They are indifferent to the de-

struction of the creation they say they believe God made. And because their faith is unmoored but their religious impulse is strong, they seek a replacement for religion. This is why they could suddenly rally to a cult called Trump. He may be the least Christian person in America, but his persona met the religious need their own faiths had ceased to provide. The terrible truth of the last three years is that the fresh appeal of a leader-cult has overwhelmed the fading truths of Christianity.

And critiquing the humorlessness of the Left, he says,

> And so the young adherents of the Great Awokening exhibit the zeal of the Great Awakening. . . . [They] punish heresy by banishing sinners from society or coercing them to public demonstrations of shame, and provide an avenue for redemption in the form of a thorough public confession of sin. "Social justice" theory requires the admission of white privilege in ways that are strikingly like the admission of original sin. A Christian is born again; an activist gets woke. To the belief in human progress unfolding through history—itself a remnant of Christian eschatology—it adds the Leninist twist of a cadre of heroes who jump-start the revolution.[1]

If Christianity in America has indeed become a joke, then at the core of this disheartening development is our failure to rightly understand what Christianity *is*. For the apostle Paul, the message about Jesus was a scandal (Gk. *skandalon*, 1 Cor. 1:23). It was, it is, when rightly understood, a stumbling block, foolishness, a scandal to the powers that be.

Ironically, the good news of Jesus has itself been scandalized in today's America. The scandal that once was seems long forgotten. Now the scandal of Christianity is its bastardization. We must

---

1. Andrew Sullivan, "America's New Religions," *Intelligencer*, December 7, 2018, http://nymag.com/intelligencer/2018/12/andrew-sullivan-americas-new-religions.html.

find some way to strip away the facades, acknowledge the ways we have illegitimately scandalized the gospel, and witness anew to the rightful scandal of the reconciling work of God in our midst.

We must deconstruct our own paltry notions about what Christianity itself is and come anew to the conviction that Christianity is not a *religion*. It is a *politic*. Tragically few people—including the majority of Christians, whether liberal or conservative—recognize Christianity as a politic. I am not suggesting the more palatable notion merely that Christianity has political implications. I am suggesting that it is itself a politic, which has an all-encompassing vision of human history.

While more will be said later, suffice it here simply to say that by *politic* I mean an all-encompassing manner of communal life that grapples with all the questions the classical art of politics has always asked: How do we live together? How do we deal with offenses? How do we deal with money? How do we deal with enemies and violence? How do we arrange marriage and families and social structures? How is authority mediated, employed, ordered? How do we rightfully order passions and appetites? And much more besides, but most especially add these: Where is human history headed? What does it mean to be human? And what does it look like to live in a rightly ordered human community that engenders flourishing, justice, and the peace of God?

Unfortunately and in contrast, Christianity has been relegated to the socially and politically insignificant category of a private religion. This move to privatize Christian faith, thought to be the height of modern brilliance, has simply resulted in the great triumph of so-called secularism and the Western political tradition. And Christians—of both liberal and conservative stripe—have contributed to this demise of Christian witness.

To be clear, I am not advocating any sort of return to imperialist forms of Christian faith. (Nor to political prospects such as the Spanish Inquisition, Calvin's Geneva, or America's alt-right.) The problems with imperialist instances of Christian practice is *not* that they understand Christianity to be inherently political. They are wrong in allying themselves with coercive political means and such means conjoined with national or imperial borders and identities. By doing so they subvert the genius of the Jesus for whom the love of God is radically free and radically gracious, making possible (a) the political possibility that rejection and loss may be hallmarks of the kingdom of God, until the kingdom comes in fullness, but also (b) the political possibility that unfathomable and as yet unimagined possibilities are made possible by the resurrecting power of God, even before the kingdom comes in all its fullness.

NEITHER RIGHT, NOR LEFT, NOR RELIGIOUS

The question before us is whether we can even begin to articulate a vision of Christianity that is "neither right nor left nor religious." A handful of biblical commentators have noted that Jesus's temptation in the wilderness was a time of testing and discernment: Jesus was self-consciously sorting through what sort of Messiah, what sort of Anointed One, he would be. It is deeply ironic, though not funny, that so much of the Christian tradition, especially in America, has opted for one of the three means offered up by the devil.

Jesus Was Tempted to Take Up the Way of MAGA

The cult of greatness and imperialist power is explicitly rejected in the New Testament, tantamount to "bowing down to Satan." To make the nation "great" is a subtle and powerful temptation. The so-called liberals who castigate the so-called conservatives for their unprincipled hankering after power often act as if we are dealing with a categorically different time. In fact, we are not. Of course things seem different because the patina of common decency and the respect for social mores has been removed. The vulgarity, demeaning speech, and shameless greed are shocking. But these days do not in fact represent some new book of human history; it is but a quite ugly new chapter in a very old book, the tale in which Christians lust for the coercive power of the state in service to a supposedly Christian agenda.

It is indeed an old and a sorry tale—one which the haters of Christianity love to tell, and they have good reasons for doing so because of the mischief and loss of life resulting from imperialist Christians: the great Christian king of the Franks, Charlemagne, who would allow the pagan Saxons either to be baptized or to be killed; John Calvin, who would vote for the execution of Michael Servetus as punishment for his heresy; the horrors of the Spanish conquistadores who brought Christianity to the Americas along with their gruesome attack dogs and killing of mothers and butchering of children; or even Harry Truman, a Christian who loved the Sermon on the Mount but remains the only head of state in human history to have dropped an atomic weapon on civilian populations.

This sort of satanic temptation inevitably leads to loss for both church and world.

Jesus Was Tempted to Become a Religious Reformer

The faith is not about politics, says this option. No, it's about proper religion; it's about *spirituality* and *saving souls*. Similarly, in our own day we continue to have those who are more interested in religion than politics. "Politics is unimportant," they say. Then follows pietistic pablum: "God's got this," they go on with a gleaming smile, insisting that "temporal things do not matter, for only eternal things matter."

But such assertions are the stock-in-trade of the wealthy and the privileged.

The poor and the marginalized know money and politics matter. Slaves in Tennessee in 1862 knew politics matters, as did the women of Tennessee in 1920. Pennsylvania steel workers in 1892, Oklahoma dust-bowl families in 1937, California farm workers in 1960, black Mississippi students in 1964, Kent State students in

1970—they all knew that politics and money matter, inextricably woven into the difference between flourishing and floundering and are often the difference between life and death.

Biblically considered, the Hebrew slaves knew politics and money matter, too. Moses did not come to them to admonish them to be patient until the coming of the "sweet by-and-by." Moses did not say, "Yes, life's a bitch, but get right with the Lord, and when you die, you'll get your eternal reward in heaven."

No, he most certainly did not. Instead, Moses went to pharaoh. The prophet went to the powermonger and said in no uncertain terms, "Let my people go." In the same way, when Jesus announced his agenda in the shadow of the greatest superpower of his day, he proclaimed,

> The Spirit of the Lord is upon me,
>> because he has anointed me to bring good news to the
>> poor.
> He has sent me to proclaim release to the captives
>> and recovery of sight to the blind,
>> to let the oppressed go free,
>> to proclaim the year of the Lord's favor.
>
> (Luke 4:18–19)

Jesus Was Tempted to Reduce His Work to Social Activism

The Gospel of John recounts that when Jesus did in fact feed the multitudes, they sought to make him king. He slipped away to avoid their agenda. What of this today? The progressives are not wrong to insist that the conservatives have too often obscured the necessity of justice, working for it, bearing witness to it. In fact, they have done the church a great service by insisting that the church turn away from its systemic racism and patriarchy and homophobia and all other such social ills, which are a sickness unto death.

And yet in our day such a tendency has obscured another

undeniable and central element to the Christian tradition: we are not called to some vague spirituality made manifest in concerns for social justice. More, the legalisms and shaming of the Left are too often, in fact, a sort of perverse mirror image of their perceived enemies on the right. Let us not forget that *the Pharisees were something like first-century progressives*, while the Sadducees were something like first-century conservatives. And just as with the Pharisees, we see a tendency among the Left to draw judgments of inclusion and exclusion, public shaming, and puritanical moralisms. "He eats with sinners and publicans!" said the Pharisees of Jesus. "He eats with racists and Republicans!" might be the analogy for today.

No, neither right nor left nor religious. Instead, we have been invited to become a part of the people of God. In this sense Christianity *is* a religion and not merely a spirituality: we are called to be a people who order the whole of our lives to the goodness of God. And we are called to do so not as mere individuals but as a people gifted with the sacraments by which the grace of God nourishes us, sustains us, and allows us to become more than we could ever become on our autonomous, lonely paths.

For the witness of would-be Christians to be rehabilitated itself, we must take seriously the fourth socio-spiritual-political option, which Jesus chose as an alternative to these three temptations.

In an attempt to sketch a broad outline of what such an option might look like in our context, I lay out fifteen propositions, neither right nor left nor religious.

Or, we might say, a Christianity that is a sort of radical conservatism or a liberal orthodoxy.

Each of the fifteen chapters begins with a concise summary followed by some exposition and explanation. It may be helpful to read all fifteen concise summaries and then return to read the exposition and explanation sections.

The promise of Christ has ensured the survival of the church. But it may not be too much to suggest that if Christianity in the West is going to bear faithful witness to its Messiah, then the times are critical. I offer these propositions as a potential resource for faithful witness in these critical times.

FAITHFUL WITNESS IN CRITICAL TIMES

These propositions will inevitably leave you with a great host of questions, many of which I continue to struggle with. But it is in having a different set of questions that we may bring some new good news to bear upon our political context. In that vein I would suggest that this manifesto is, in another sense, a sort of syllabus for the sort of study Christians in the West must do to reconfigure our faith as good news to the world instead of the paltry, partisan, privatized matter too often proffered.

A note of qualification: I do not see any of these fifteen propositions as original, some new discovery about the nature of Christian conviction. Instead, they are all quite—so it seems to me—noncontroversial assertions, simple restatements of orthodox Christianity. While I do hope that my arrangement and communication of them provide a creative and compelling picture, I am more concerned simply that these convictions be communicated clearly. The fact that some of this material may appear controversial illustrates how desperately we would-be Christians need to be reminded of the basic claims of our faith and how deep is the captivity of Christianity in America, a captivity that is very often one of our own making.

And finally, I would like to add two words of encouragement. First, do not be afraid. If indeed John's Jesus be true—"you shall know the truth, and the truth shall set you free"—then do not be afraid. By choosing to tell different stories, make different observations, ask different sorts of questions, you have an immense power to change the nature of political discourse in your community. Though some—whether right, left, or religious—may find many of these contentions as threatening (or tacky), do not be afraid. Be of good courage. If we would be Christians, then we must, with kindness and winsome speech, say the things, embody the things, that

9

too few are saying or doing. We must show up—at dinner tables, in worship gatherings, on the public square, in the boardroom—with a nonanxious presence, with a deep clarity regarding our identity, story, and convictions. And we may be surprised again how the Spirit of God may rekindle the gospel in our midst.

Second, remember too the primary posture of the church in the world is constructive instead of critical. The prophetic voice in the Old Testament, with its notes of indictment and critique, is primarily an inside voice, not in the sense of quiet, certainly, but in the sense that the Hebrew prophets spoke their judgment to the people of the covenant, those who *should have known better*. The kerygmatic voice, the proclamation of good news in the New Testament, is the primary outside voice. The outside voice is our posture of reconciliation, becoming "all things to all people" so that some may come to know Christ. There undoubtedly will be points at which our existence as the church entails a certain judgment upon the world. But such judgment should ordinarily be implicit, drawn naturally out of the contrast between the way of life of the church and those outside the church. Our task is to be salt and light; these days, the world may not need more critics.

For additional materials of study, reflection, or engagement, please visit www.LeeCCamp.com/scandalous.

History Is Not One Damn Thing after Another

SUMMARY

A first step in finding a politic which is "neither right nor left nor religious" is construing *history* correctly. For some, "history is just one damn thing after another." This famed phrase well depicts those who believe history has no meaning, no direction or goal, no ultimate purpose.

Many Christians also think this: "It's all going to burn, and none of this matters." What matters, they say, is the human soul "going to heaven when we die." No need to concern ourselves with troubling social or political matters because "God's got this." Politics and social affairs are of no concern to the faithful.

Many Jews, Muslims, and Christians know better. Some prominent early Christians, in fact, believed such spiritualizing to be a grave heresy that would destroy the Christian faith. They saw human history as the stage for the unfolding of the drama of God's work. In this drama God was assured to be the victor, even if God's ways are often inscrutable, even exasperating to those who love God. This God who had created a good creation would restore it, redeem it, save it. This God would set right the injustice and violence, remove the arrogant mighty ones from their throne rooms and White Houses, fill up the hungry, and bind up the oppressed.

In this drama some humans, feeble and petty as they may

be, ally themselves for the work of God. Meanwhile, many of the preening, arrogant powers array themselves against both God and humankind. Those arrogant powers often serve as the handmaidens of death, while the God of life keeps intruding, or so it appears to the powers, bringing light into the darkness.

But human history is not one damn meaningless thing after another, even if the horror of the mundane evil propagated by the powers tempts us to despair. History has a *goal*, a direction toward a climax: the author of life shall write a tale, has written a tale, in which all lies and greed and ugliness and war; prisons and lusts, oppression and hate; hostility, disease, contempt, and envy; all shall be undone and set right, and there shall come a triumph of truth and goodness and beauty, which no ear has yet heard, and no eye has yet seen.

EXPOSITION

The Scream has been called the *Mona Lisa* of the twentieth century. Edvard Munch's iconic painting arose from a dreadful vision he had one day at sunset. Walking along a fjord in his native Norway, he said he "sensed an infinite scream passing through nature." That scream captures the modern sense of despair, in which no hope remains, only anxiety, loneliness, and despondency.

Munch's artistic angst illustrates well some common philosophical convictions about history: that history has no direction or is merely an endless cycle of repetition or is but one damn meaningless thing after another. There are also religions, supposedly Christian versions of such, that think that human history is ultimately unimportant. These alleged Christian versions postulate some hope, some purpose, but it is a purpose beyond history, outside of history. It is a reward "up there," souls floating off to heaven. "Our true home," they say, "is in heaven. We need not concern ourselves with social or political or historical matters."

Edvard Munch, *The Scream*, 1893, oil, tempera, and pastel on card-board, 91 x 73 cm, National Gallery of Norway. *Wikimedia Commons*

One therapeutic solution to Munch's *Scream* is simply not to look too closely at history, not get ourselves involved in matters that don't concern us in our spiritual contentment. If you don't pay attention to the death camps or the brokenness of the cities or the systemic greed undergirding our economies, then you need not feel the despair. You simply ignore it, look beyond, to the sweet by-and-by.

This is Marx's classical critique: religion as the opiate of the masses.

But as much biblical scholarship has been contending of late, "going to heaven" is *not* the point of the New Testament, nor did early Christians believe it so.

Along with recent biblical scholarship, the poets and prophets and song-singers have always known better. The Hebrew prophets envisioned a day in which "the lamb shall lie down with the lion," "the nations shall learn war no more," and "swords shall be beaten into plowshares." The poets and lyricists of our own day insist that "a change is gonna come" and that we "still haven't found what [we're] looking for." And Martin Luther King Jr. proclaimed that he had a dream and that "the arc of history is long, but it bends toward justice."

All these poetic utterances point us toward hopefulness. Each assumes that history is not, in the final analysis, a meaningless morass of vanity. Instead, history has a direction: injustice undone, brokenness bound up, captivity taken captive. This is the goal of history, the end of history. We need not confuse "end of history" with the termination of time; it is, rather, best considered as the final goal toward which all things are moving.[1]

Historic Christianity insists precisely this: that history is headed toward a glorious re-creation the likes of which only poets can begin to voice.

This conviction is a most significant starting point for considering a sociopolitical vision for Christian practice.

---

1. A great deal of work is currently being done in the West on how to make sense of the Christian doctrine of original sin given the now-pervasive acceptance of the theory of evolution and the rise of the human species by means of natural selection. Much of this work appears fruitful. It is not as clear to me that similar work is being done with regard to Christian eschatological teaching, given new insights in cosmology and theories of relativity and the like, but this seems needful as well.

Hope as an Interpretation of History

This idea—a goal of history—entails the notion of *hope.*

This is where the American myth and Christian teaching have a high degree of overlap: both assert the notion of a direction to history and thus the practical importance of *hope.* There is similar overlap with the secularist who speaks of progress, assuming some direction in human history.[2] As the philosopher John Gray describes John Stuart Mill, one of the preeminent philosophers of the liberal tradition in the West: "he founded an orthodoxy—the belief in improvement that is the unthinking faith of people who think they have no religion."[3]

If it is true that Christianity does proclaim that history matters and is going somewhere, then it turns out that many American and secularist forms of hope are *more Christian* than the otherworldly dreams of some Christians. Or, at a minimum, we can say that such Americans and secularists are more Christian in their conviction regarding the immeasurable worth of the whole of human history.

When Americans and secularists insist that history mat-

2. In his typical provocative and insightful fashion, Andrew Sullivan notes that we all have a "religion" these days, even the atheists, in some attenuated fashion, and he explicitly draws the parallel between Christian faith and the secularist progress myth: "Seduced by scientism, distracted by materialism, insulated, like no humans before us, from the vicissitudes of sickness and the ubiquity of early death, the post-Christian West believes instead in something we have called progress—a gradual ascent of mankind toward reason, peace, and prosperity—as a substitute in many ways for our previous monotheism. We have constructed a capitalist system that turns individual selfishness into a collective asset and showers us with earthly goods; we have leveraged science for our own health and comfort. Our ability to extend this material bonanza to more and more people is how we define progress; and progress is what we call meaning." Andrew Sullivan, "America's New Religions," *Intelligencer,* December 7, 2018, http://nymag.com/intelligencer/2018/12/andrew-sullivan-americas-new-religions.html.

3. John Gray, *Seven Types of Atheism* (New York: Farrar, Straus & Giroux, 2018), 36

ters—that social policy and scientific concern for the earth *matter*, that economic policy and staggering disparities in wealth *matter*, that the industrialization of war and imprisonment for profit *matter*—they show themselves, in this regard, more Christian than many Christians.

The hope of heaven, in other words, too easily becomes an *ahistorical* hope, a hope that cares nothing for the unfolding of the human drama, except perhaps to hope that sufficient religious or moral choices are rightly made so that the soul can sweep through the Pearly Gates.

In this way, *some American revivalists may have done more to undermine Christianity in America than the secularists* by making the locus of Christianity the individual's judgment before the throne of God, a religion that has little to say to the teeming and throbbing pain of human history and instead calls us to cast our vision to an afterlife removed from care for human history or for God's good creation. Such a tendency contributed to Malcolm X renouncing Christianity and embracing Islam. "The white man has taught us to shout and sing and pray until we die, to wait until *death*, for some dreamy heaven-in-the-hereafter, when we're *dead*, while this white man has milk and honey in the streets paved with golden dollars right here on *this* earth!"[4]

One of the failings of the secularist notion of progress is its vague lack of content: What does progress entail? What does it look like? What is its content?

Similarly, the Christian notion of hope must attend to these same questions. The biblical creation account, in which Jews and Christians maintain that the creation itself is *good*, is indispensable in beginning to answer such questions. The Genesis account about creation is not a sort of crypto-scientific description best read as a literal account of the unfolding of the cosmos. Instead, the Genesis account insists on the moral and aesthetic goodness of the creation grounded and rooted in the

4. Malcolm X and Alex Haley, *The Autobiography of Malcolm X* (1964; repr., New York: Ballantine Books, 2015), 224.

abundant generosity of God. It presumes a community inherent in the very nature of God and that this self-giving God invited all creation, and humankind in a special way, to participate in the joyous work of tilling and cultivating in the unfolding story of the garden of God.

And yet death and death's handmaidens duped the humans, vandalizing the abode of God and humankind. And yet more, this God who is good and patient and long-suffering did not leave humankind to its own devices but would act in love and power and justice to set things right—while still honoring humankind's radical freedom to reject the good ways of God—to free humankind from the bondage in which it found itself.

"New heavens and new earth"—that's what one of the prophets called the greatly anticipated redemption of God. Christianity was not concerned first and foremost with some realm of disembodied spirits beyond the pale of human history.

Consider the stunning objection of one of the early church martyrs, Justin. He was arrested and beheaded for his faith. His commentary is striking. There are some "who are called Christians," he said rather derisively, who insisted that "their souls, when they die, are taken to heaven." He classified such people among "godless, impious heretics."[5]

This is an ironic, odd reality: that an early defender of Christianity who refused to submit to the demands of the Roman Empire, who insisted that Jesus was Lord, and who was executed for his stance, would say that our American Joe Christian is not in fact a Christian but a heretic. Justin was not executed because he was religious. He was executed because he held to a competing interpretation of human history. Justin held to an alternative politic that entailed that the Word of God revealed in this Jesus of Nazareth was the only rational explanation that made sense of our lives and was the only rational ground for hope. The resurrecting power of

---

5. Justin Martyr, *Dialogue with Trypho*, 80, Ante-Nicene Fathers, ed. Alexander Roberts and James Donaldson (1885; repr., Peabody, MA: Hendrickson, 1996).

God which had raised this Jesus from the dead would not only raise all of us but also make new the heavens and the earth and set all things right.

Jesus and other early Christians were not executed because they were spiritual. They were executed because their politic was a threat to the powers that be.

The Content of the Hope

It is not the afterlife for which the prophet longs but the setting right of this life: the pain of lost loves and the death of infants, of old griefs and deep regret, of the weeping of mothers or the cries of war. All shall be wrought up into the work of this God who shall wipe away every tear from every eye and make all things right.

Hear, for example, the Hebrew prophet Isaiah:

> For I am about to create new heavens
> and a new earth;
> the former things shall not be remembered
> or come to mind.
> But be glad and rejoice forever
> in what I am creating;
> for I am about to create Jerusalem as a joy,
> and its people as a delight.
> I will rejoice in Jerusalem,
> and delight in my people;
> no more shall the sound of weeping be heard in it,
> or the cry of distress.
> No more shall there be in it
> an infant that lives but a few days,
> or an old person who does not live out a lifetime;
> for one who dies at a hundred years will be considered a youth,
> and one who falls short of a hundred will be considered
> accursed.

They shall build houses and inhabit them;
    they shall plant vineyards and eat their fruit.
They shall not build and another inhabit;
    they shall not plant and another eat;
for like the days of a tree shall the days of my people be,
    and my chosen shall long enjoy the work of their hands.
They shall not labor in vain,
    or bear children for calamity;
for they shall be offspring blessed by the LORD—
    and their descendants as well.
Before they call I will answer,
    while they are yet speaking I will hear.
The wolf and the lamb shall feed together,
    the lion shall eat straw like the ox;
    but the serpent—its food shall be dust!
They shall not hurt or destroy
    on all my holy mountain,
    says the LORD. (Isa. 65:17–25)

A great abundance of many of the finest lines of poetry inscribed in human history is grasping after, longing after, painting a glimpse of this coming hope. The street of gold, God wiping every tear from every eye, the great river that flows from the throne of God lined on both banks with the very tree of life—all these poetic images of the triumph of God—are *not depicted in heaven* in the biblical text. Instead, Revelation 21–22 depict such glory occurring *here*, even here in the midst of human history, even here in the midst of us. Oppression shall be undone, infidelity cast out, captivity itself taken captive, not in the sweet by-and-by but in the climax of the story of God in our midst.

The biblical vision, then, will countenance no supposed withdrawal from politics. The prophets will hear none of this religious pretending that history does not matter, all in the name of a pietistic assertion that "God's got this." The biblical texts refuse to minimize the importance of social and historical developments, will not look the other way as the scoundrels of death vandalize and terrorize, will not let us look away from the bitter cries of mothers, the lonely privation of old men, the needless deaths of children.

No! "Captivity has been taken captive." "Let my people go!" "Let justice roll down like waters, and righteousness like an ever-flowing stream." "Do justice, love mercy, and walk humbly with God!"

The great paradigmatic moment of political encounter in the founding narrative of the Christians comes with the gospel: "Change, and believe in the good news of the reign of God." This new political movement of God would entail specific practices unlike those of the nations, unlike those of the powers whom we have falsely assumed have the monopoly on political power. This new political movement would offer the world something at which kings and rulers would shake their heads: love of enemies, practices of reconciliation, sharing of wealth, honoring of marriage, renunciation of our varied practices of greed and lust, and an embrace of all the practices of life and mercy and kindness.

Or thus said Jesus.

In all these and many compelling ways besides, the Scriptures call us to face the pain and brokenness of human history.

And we are called to have the courage to play our part: to be brave as the soldier, committed as the activist, devoted as the evangelical, sedulous as the journalist—speaking to, acting for, sowing the seeds of the world that is on its way, knowing that it requires great labor, perseverance, and a willingness to suffer, and promises, too, on the journey, of deep joy and gladness, friends and fellow pilgrims, called as we are to be bearers of the end of history. We shall refuse to vindicate Marx by refusing to let our faith be an opiate of the masses; we shall face the pain and oppression squarely and proclaim the good news that the hope of all humankind, evoked in and out of our tears and cries and confusion and anger, has come, shall come. And we shall dare to live by it.

So: No, history is not one damn meaningless thing after another. Moses, the prophets, and Jesus, each in their own way, insisted that history has a goal, a direction, an intrinsic and inescapable importance in the purposes of the Creator of all things good. And woe be unto those who stand in the way of this great God's unfolding of this narrative, which will not be stopped until all that is beautiful and good and true is made manifest in our midst.

The End of History Has Already Begun

SUMMARY

As noted, Christianity, Judaism, and Islam all share the important conviction that history has a goal and direction. While the particulars may vary, this *end* of history entails the righting of wrongs, setting all things to rights.

A second step in configuring a Christianity that is "neither right nor left nor religious" is found precisely at the place where Christianity, Judaism, and Islam *differ*: Christianity proclaims that Jesus of Nazareth inaugurated the end of history for which Christianity, Judaism, and Islam all wait. Judaism and Islam reject this.

Consequently, we may better understand Christianity by calling it an *interpretation* of history instead of a religion. For Christians the resurrection of the crucified Christ is the central historical claim on which Christians stake their lives: it *ushers in* the end of history, *vindicates* the way of Christ, and *inaugurates* a new political possibility in the world. We are invited by the resurrected Christ to live according to the end of history already inaugurated, but not yet fully realized, not yet consummated.

The claims of this Christ are further vindicated by a community that lives by his ways—and yet this simultaneously poses a grave threat to Christianity, in that Christians, in their failures, may become the greatest threat to their own faith.

EXPOSITION

Central to Christian faith is an assertion that history is not one meaningless thing after another, is the notion that history has a direction and a goal, and that this goal is not located external to the creation and cosmos itself but is in fact a "new heaven and new earth," a new reality. The prophets and poets, singers and songwriters have sought to find words and lyrics that may sustain such longing. Because this coming reality must be more than we can yet imagine in the particulars. Consequently, Christians sing songs and write poems and recite the words of the prophets of old.

Christians are not an exclusive club with regard to the conviction that history has a discernible direction. Many Americans and secularists, capitalists and communists, Muslims and Jews may have little disagreement with Christians about history having a goal and direction. (There are others, such as many ideologically oriented evolutionists, who do not believe that history has such a purpose, such a direction.)

But there is an important difference among these who share the conviction that history has a purpose; Christianity claims that the end of history *has been inaugurated*. This is a key distinction with other so-called historic religions such as Judaism or Islam: namely, the claim that the end of history has already begun. Christians believe that the glorious reign of God has already broken into human history, has been inaugurated.

This claim provides a fruitful interpretive lens through which to read the New Testament. Consider in this way the Gospel stories such as the healing of disease, the forgiveness of offenses, the reconciliation of enemies, the sharing of wealth, the learning of the ways of peace, the triumph of life over death. All these are but the end of history intruding upon the present. A child sick unto death taken up from her bed whole is but the firstfruits of the end of history. An agent of empire distributing his ill-gotten wealth to the poor is but an outpouring of the goal of history. A right-wing conservative and a leftist radical sitting at the same table sharing bread and wine together is but a foretaste of the reconciliation of all things.

Edward Hicks, *The Peaceable Kingdom*, ca. 1834, oil on canvas, National Gallery of Art. *Wikimedia Commons*

In the same way, this claim regarding the inauguration of the end of history provides a fruitful interpretive lens through which to read the apostle Paul. He seems at first glance to speak out of both sides of his mouth, speaking at one moment of salvation having already occurred and at other moments as if we wait for God's salvation. But suddenly such doublespeak seems altogether plausible if we have at hand this lens of a kingdom inaugurated but not yet consummated.

So What? This: To Live Proleptically

So what is the importance of this emphasis on an inaugurated kingdom?

This: *the inaugurated kingdom of God provides a proleptic political stance.*

Proleptic is a grammatical term in which a future event is so sure to come, so sure to be the case, that it is spoken of in the present tense. As an illustration, when our boys were young, I was ready one morning to drive them to school. Standing in the kitchen with our ten-year-old second-born, David, I shouted up the stairs to his older brother, "Chandler, I'm in the car." David quietly replied, "No you're not Dad. You're standing in the kitchen."

"David," I replied impatiently, "that was a *proleptic* statement. It was a proleptic statement."

So sure of what was to come, even if still in the future, I spoke of it in the present tense. This is the proleptic voice. It is one way of describing the vocation of the Christian church in the world. It is the key to Christian ethics and indeed the key to understanding much of the New Testament text itself. Christian discipleship calls us to a proleptic stance in which we embody and bear witness to the world that is coming. We labor *now*, plowing and sowing and watering and reaping the varied firstfruits of that still-coming kingdom.

The coming kingdom entails a shared abundance and unencumbered generosity; thus we practice generosity and hospitality even now, in the present. The coming kingdom entails the unlearning of war; thus we learn the councils of peace now. The coming kingdom entails the righting of all wrongs by truth telling and suffering love; thus we tell the truth, practice suffering love, and right wrongs now.

In contrast, political realism assumes that the brokenness of the world is most real. The political realist insists that interests must always be balanced by counterinterests, and coercive power must always be checked by countercoercive power, and when "necessary," that threats be checked by the threat of or actual employment of violence.

But the gospel claim—that the kingdom of God has been inaugurated—redefines *reality*. It redefines what is most real.

What is most real is not the scheming of tyrants or the lies of those in power. What is most real is not that might makes right or that greatness is defined by the size of one's arsenal. What is most real, we Christians claim, is the power of God revealed in one who suffers in love and trusts that right has been made right not through might but through mercy, repentance, and resurrection.

This new reality fundamentally reorders the ways of life and death, politics and power. The significance of this claim is hard to overstate. It makes all the difference in whether we Christians do, in fact, understand our own faith.

In the days of the rise of the Third Reich, many Christians were celebrating the rise of Hitler and his conservative family values. Knowing that a great evil had come upon the land and sensing the need to train pastors in such a way that they could withstand the onslaught of Nazi propaganda and its threat to Christianity in Germany, Dietrich Bonhoeffer convened an illegal seminary in Finkenwalde.

One of Bonhoeffer's underground seminary students later reported, "Twice [Bonhoeffer] quoted to them the words: 'One man asks: What is to come? The other: What is right? And that,'" said Bonhoeffer, "'is the difference between the free man and the slave.'"[1]

Christianity is no slave religion. It is a politic of authentic freedom grounded in the confidence that even death itself has been overcome and that we may, even now, live in proleptic anticipation of its consummate triumph.

The Resurrection of the Dead

Christianity proclaims that Jesus of Nazareth, crucified under Pontius Pilate, was raised bodily from the dead. Moreover, we proclaim that Easter shall become a universal historical event.

The resurrection of Jesus is not a merely religious claim. The resurrection of Jesus is an inherently *political* claim. To say that the dead shall be resurrected is not a claim about "going to heaven." It

---

1. Cited in Mark Devine, *Bonhoeffer Speaks Today: Following Jesus at All Costs* (Nashville: Broadman & Holman, 2005), 48.

is a claim, first and foremost, that the kingdom of God has been inaugurated and that the imperialist arrogance that humiliated and tortured the Son has been overcome such that the ways of the Son are honored in glorious vindication.

The resurrection is a twofold political statement made by the Creator of all things:

Behold the triumph of life over all the powers of death!
Behold the manner and means of the triumph!

And behold this man upon the cross, whom the power brokers humiliated and the pious dismissed! Behold this man who loved even unto death and forgave even those who despitefully used him, who prayed for those who persecuted him! Behold this man who called the weary and heavy-laden, who welcomed children and honored the prostitute, who dined with the poor and despised the imperialists and the mighty, the tax collectors and the patriots, calling all to the goodness and freedom and brilliance of the new order of the ages, which has come among you! Though we despised him, mocked him, beat him, killed him, no grave can hold down either his body or his beauty! Behold this man raised from the dead! The long-awaited end of human history has come upon us, has broken into our very midst! See and believe and receive the glorious goal of history into our midst. Know the truth and be free with liberty glorious in its delights, and possibilities, and abundance.

Justin Martyr, as noted in the discussion of proposition 1, castigated those Christians who say that our souls, when we die, are taken off to heaven. These "say there is no resurrection of the dead, and that their souls, when they die, are taken to heaven." It is these whom Justin calls "godless, impious heretics" and insists that we ought "not imagine that they are Christians." "I and others, who are right-minded Christians on all points," he goes on, "are assured that there will be a resurrection of the dead."[2]

---

2. Justin Martyr, *Dialogue with Trypho*, 80, Ante-Nicene Fathers, ed. Alexander Roberts and James Donaldson (1885; repr., Peabody, MA: Hendrickson, 1996).

To reduce Christianity to an afterlife religion, to reduce it to some spiritual escape from real life and history, this was to pervert Christianity and fundamentally misconstrue it. The doctrine of resurrection is a claim that the "end of history" has been inaugurated. Just as a presidential inauguration begins a new administration, just as the Revolutionary War inaugurated the political entity called the United States, and just as a commencement ceremony launches a graduate into a new season of life, so the resurrection of Christ inaugurates the triumph of all the forces of life and justice and goodness over the fallen forces of death and oppression and slavery.

To sum up then: Christianity is foremost a claim that the end of history has been inaugurated. And this historical claim entails a call to pledge allegiance to this new politic that has broken into human history. Christianity is, in other words, not so much a religion as it is an interpretation of history. Christianity is a claim regarding *the* meaning of history: that the *direction* and the *end* of history are all revealed in the suffering love of Christ, which has triumphed over all that which seeks to subvert the goodness of God.

But we must be careful to note that the gospel is not *merely* an interpretation of history, not merely an academic or pedantic assertion about how to interpret the unfolding of historical data. It is an interpretation that carries with it a new power and is thus itself a *history-making force* set loose in the world.[3]

The Evidence?

Obviously, these are contentious claims.

However, the sort of interpretation of Christianity advocated here becomes testable in at least some facets by empirical data. It becomes subject to pragmatic review and practical critique.

Take for example those early Jewish and pagan critics of Christianity who rejected Jesus as the Messiah. Jesus could not be the

3. Cf. William Stringfellow, *A Private and Public Faith* (Grand Rapids: Eerdmans, 1962), 62.

Messiah, they insisted, because human history still exhibited a long sorry trail of grief. "Your own prophets," they said in effect, "insist that when Messiah comes the nations will learn war no more. And look, you dumb fools, the nations continue to wage war. The most elementary observations lead us therefore to reject Jesus as Messiah."

The critics raised, in other words, what we might call an evidentiary problem. Here they were not asking for evidence of a body raised from the dead centuries earlier. They were asking for evidence in the unfolding narrative of human history that legitimated the Christians' historical and political claims. You claim Jesus is the Messiah to bring peace to the world? Where is this peace? Do you not see the war making and hostility that continue to pervade human history?

Numerous of the early church fathers responded, in effect, this way: "You are wrong. Jesus is the Messiah. The evidence? This: we the people of God who claim Jesus as Messiah, comprising people of every tribe, tongue, and land, once made war with one another and lived in hostility one with the other. We now have put away war and embody in our common life the peace of God. We share our lives and possessions; we forgive offenses and bear one another's burdens; we celebrate and honor the life of the marginalized and the poor and the outcast; and we live in a freedom which otherwise makes no sense."[4]

For these early Christians the political and historical shape of their common life was central to the claim that Jesus is Lord. Their apologetic, their defense of the claim that Jesus is Lord, was grounded in their new political way of being in the world.

While such an apologetic may be compelling, this sword may cut in two directions. If the Christian way of life can be employed to argue for the claim that Jesus is the Messiah, then failures of

---

4. See the discussion in John Driver, *How Christians Made Peace with War* (Scottdale, PA: Herald Press, 1988), chap. 1. I discuss this at more length in *Mere Discipleship: Radical Christianity in a Rebellious World*, 2nd ed. (Grand Rapids: Brazos Press, 2008), chap. 11.

the Christian church can be employed to reject the claim of Jesus as Messiah. Contemporary critics may say to Christians in the West what critics said to early Christians two millennia ago: based on your own texts, Jesus could not be the Messiah, for we live in days still riddled with violence and hostility and patriarchy, the gap between wealth and poor growing at an inconceivable rate, the mighty accumulating weapons inconceivable in days gone by.

Such a critique may indeed be devastating to the contemporary Christian church. By and large, the Christian church in the West in the early twenty-first century cannot reply as did the second- and third-century church. More, our cultured and educated despisers may say to us: Look! Not only are our days violent and hostile, but it is the Christians who propagate and prop up and celebrate such militancy, such hostile nationalism, such imperialist might!

It is a sad state of affairs. Insufficient data may be found among Christians to confirm that Christianity is true, and consequently we Christians may be among the primary players responsible for the rapid rejection of Christian faith in the West, not the secularists, not the liberals, not the conservatives, not the Americans, not the communists. "Judgment must begin with the household of God."

How have we found ourselves in this mess? One plausible interpretation runs this way:

1. We bought into the Western notion that religion is a private affair, unrelated to politics and history and sociology.
2. But knowing that history and politics and social structures still matter a great deal, we cast about to find some bearer of historical meaning.
3. Not finding it then (as we had already supposed) in Christianity, we yielded this role to the nation-state, as the primary player in the unfolding of history.
4. Finally, convinced of the importance of being politically and socially relevant, we had to get on the side of the right (that is, "correct") political partisan agenda, nation-state, or power-mongering entity.

It is not the final step of these four that is a dangerous rejection of Christianity. Instead, each successive step gives up something inherent to the historic Christian faith, and with each successive step we give up the basics of elementary Christian orthodoxy.

But it would be grossly unfair—on either the part of the cultured despisers of Christianity or on the part of the internal critics of Christianity—to fail to note the marked exceptions. There remain sparks of light enkindling our faith: the mothers in Charleston who in the midst of their grief spoke reconciliation to the murderer who had invaded their church; William Wilberforce, who exhausted his life in Parliament in the quest to abolish slavery in the United Kingdom; Nelson Mandela, who found that his own unjust suffering gave rise to an immense power of reconciliation and capacity to work for justice. And many, many more.

One more complicating factor to note on the evidentiary problem before we conclude proposition 2: the end of the story has not yet come. To claim that a new movement has been inaugurated in human history and thus to look for evidence for such an inauguration is an altogether legitimate matter. But to note that we are still in the midst of the story means there remain a vast number of possibilities as to where this story shall go before it reaches the end. We know full well that epic sagas have many dark days, some so dark that we cannot envision how any satisfying end may result. And we know full well that the work of God is often like leaven in bread, like seed sown in a field, and we may not be able to see all the work that is going on in the secret recesses of human culture and history.

And just as we cannot judge a book by its cover, we also cannot judge well a book without reading all the way to the end. In the same way, we cannot fully judge well any interpretation of human history that purports to know where it is headed—at least we cannot judge well any such interpretation—until history itself will vindicate or vanquish the interpreter. And all this is to say that to live proleptically is a risky affair. (So the Old Testament, for example, commends us to judge those prophets who make future predictions this way: Did things turn out the way the self-proclaimed prophet prophesied? If so, then you have a true prophet. If not, then you have a false prophet.)

While living proleptically is a truly risky affair for us would-be Christians, this does not mean that there are others who have somehow found a nonrisky manner of living. All who live by the conviction that they know where history is headed—whether they be American patriots, ideological capitalists, devoted communists, pious Jews, or the most committed secularist lover of progress— are taking a risk, based on their interpretation of history. In other words, this is a practical problem for everyone who lives by any notion of hope, progress, or longing. The risk entailed in living with the conviction that history matters, that there is a purposeful end of history, is no small matter. We may be wrong.

So, to live by the claim that history has a direction is a risky affair. And to live by the further claim that the end of history has been inaugurated in the suffering love and resurrection of Christ is risky yet again. To live by faith, to live proleptically, entails risking that resurrection and life have broken into human history, captivity taken captive by this man upon the cross, and that we are thus free to live accordingly, by love and mercy and graciousness ourselves.

It is risky not to do so, too.

But in any case, to depict Christianity as a risky political claim begins our task of staking out, in bold terms, the potential threat— and immense service—which Christian faith poses, when rightly understood and practiced, to even the most American of dreams.

American Hope Is a Bastard

SUMMARY

A sexual metaphor proves helpful. When "America" forces himself on "Hope," a bastardized form of Christian hope is born. When America forces himself into an intimate, consummating relationship with the Christian eschatological vision, we are left with an illegitimate form of Christian hope. The consummation of the eschaton is rightfully and only the province of God. No nation-state, no human actor, no social or political party—including the church of God—may take upon itself the role of consummating the hopes for which we long. Too often America and its leaders have arrogated to themselves such a role, and the bastardized forms of hope have wreaked much mischief and at times much horrific violence.

EXPOSITION

In 1980, on the eve of his election, US President Ronald Reagan said,

> I have quoted John Winthrop's words more than once on the campaign trail this year—for I believe that Americans in 1980 are every bit as committed to that vision of a shining "city on a hill," as were those long ago settlers. . . .

These visitors to that city on the Potomac do not come as white or black, red or yellow; they are not Jews or Christians; conservatives or liberals; or Democrats or Republicans. They are Americans awed by what has gone before, proud of what for them is still . . . a shining city on a hill.[1]

And in 1989, in his farewell speech, Reagan said,

I've spoken of the shining city all my political life, but I don't know if I ever quite communicated what I saw when I said it. But in my mind it was a tall proud city built on rocks stronger than oceans, wind-swept, God-blessed, and teeming with people of all kinds living in harmony and peace; a city with free ports that hummed with commerce and creativity. And if there had to be city walls, the walls had doors and the doors were open to anyone with the will and the heart to get here. That's how I saw it and see it still.[2]

Reagan's rhetoric is striking and brilliant, mixing Jesus's description of the kingdom of heaven in the Sermon on the Mount, Paul's description of the baptized community in the book of Galatians, and John's heavenly vision in the book of Revelation.

While Reagan's rhetoric is indeed brilliant, we must see it as idolatrous.

(It is important as well to note here that this critique—this charge of idolatry—is not and must not be a partisan one. Reagan here provides but a poignant example of the rhetoric often employed by the American Left and the American Right. The intention here is not to single out Reagan—for he is but one spokesperson in a long tradition of speaking in such ways, which will be developed in

1. Ronald Reagan, "Election Eve Address 'A Vision for America,'" American Presidency Project, November 3, 1980, https://www.presidency.ucsb.edu/documents/election-eve-address-vision-for-america.

2. Ronald Reagan, "Farewell Address to the Nation," Ronald Reagan Presidential Library and Museum, January 11, 1989, https://www.reaganlibrary.gov/011189i.

The New Jerusalem (**Tapestry of the Apocalypse**), **14th century.** *Kimon Berlin. Wikimedia Commons CC-BY-SA 3.0*

a subsequent chapter. The intention here is to take Reagan's rhetoric seriously and to do so from a theological perspective. Again, our task is to stake out a Christianity neither right nor left nor religious.)

Compare and contrast, then, the apostle Paul with President Reagan.

For Paul, God entrusted a ministry of reconciliation to the church. The church, rather than grounding its identity in any form of ethnic superiority or nationalism, would in fact set aside the various mechanisms of power and hostility attached to particular identities. The church comprised people of every land, tribe, ethnicity, welcoming all. The church then was called to go forth and sow seeds of reconciliation. Hostility and partisanship were to be defeated through love of enemies and doing good for those who do us wrong. For Paul, then, it was the "new humanity" created in Christ who embodied "neither Jew nor Gentile, neither slave nor free, nor is there male and female, for you are all one in Christ Jesus" (Gal. 3:28 NIV).

But for Reagan it is the "awed" citizens of the United States who "do not come as white or black, red or yellow; they are not

Jews or Christians; conservatives or liberals; or Democrats or Republicans." No, transcending all these markers of division, the Great Communicator contends, is patently *not* the fact of a unity in Christ. Transcending all these markers of presumed hostility, he claims, is the fact that "they are Americans."

For Reagan, the biblical task entrusted to the church of Jesus has been transferred to the United States. Now America is the "city on a hill." Now the task of reconciliation has been transferred to the United States. For Paul, it was the nonviolent baptized people of God who were to embody reconciled humanity. But for Reagan, it is now the United States of America, the shining city on a hill, projecting its global military might throughout the world, which is not "white or black, red or yellow." For Reagan, "they are not Jews or Christians; conservatives or liberals; or Democrats or Republicans." They are simply Americans.

Reagan weaves Paul's vision of reconciliation into John's depiction of the new Jerusalem, whose gates are always open, whose avenues and streets are filled with peoples of all the nations living in peace. Reagan's employment of this vision from the book of Revelation is done without the least embarrassment, without the least recognition of the irony.

Yet the ironies are deep and profound. Consider two examples. First, in the book of Revelation the writer John draws a sharp contrast between the mechanisms of empire and the means of the church. The imperial project—bringing about its own vision of peace, the first-century *Pax Romana*—imposes its vision by hook or by crook, by what appears to be an irresistible strength that cannot be swayed. Similarly, Reagan sought to fortify America early in his presidency with a vast buildup of military might alongside mind-boggling nuclear weapons capacities and the so-called Strategic Defense Initiative (a.k.a. "Star Wars"), which would project a sense of impenetrable power.[3] In contrast, in the book of Revela-

---

3. The Arms Control Association summarizes Reagan's endeavors this way: "Reagan's mixed legacy has permitted rival claimants to offer divergent views of his role in the end of the Cold War and the easing of nuclear tensions in

tion is the faith of the martyrs, those who would not be cowed by imperial might. They bore witness to a truth greater than empire and allowed their blood to be shed rather than bow the knee to the empire.

Second, in the book of Revelation, and indeed all of the New Testament, the "new humanity" comprises people of all nations, tribes, tongues. In this way it is the same as Reagan's vision of America. And yet here lies the rub: the new humanity of the New Testament is not bounded by artificial geographical boundaries and is not defended by military might. One of the fundamental discontinuities between Old and New Testaments lies here: the baptized community is a transboundaried people, holding passports and citizenships only as a matter of pragmatic convenience or necessity, but not as a matter of fundamental identity. But for Reagan's vision, "America," not the "new Jerusalem," is that city whose gates are always open.

Thus Reagan weaves Paul's ministry of reconciliation into John's vision of the new Jerusalem, and in a shameless *coup de grâce* co-opts Jesus's language from the Sermon on the Mount: the shining city on a hill.

Again, the ironies are deep. Jesus's shining city comprises those who weep over the injustices of human history; who are merciful with an outrageous mercy with which their God is merciful; who love their enemies and do good to those who despite-

---

the 1990s. Some facts, however, are beyond dispute. Reagan presided over a massive nuclear buildup and launched an expensive effort to build a defense against strategic missiles, which exacerbated tensions with Moscow. His military policies catalyzed widespread anti-nuclear activism that increased the political impetus for nuclear arms control. Yet, Reagan's unconventional leadership style and determination also allowed him to reach out to the Soviet leadership and relate to Gorbachev's new and bold thinking. Together the two leaders set their nations on a path toward arms control arrangements that reflected their personal abhorrence for nuclear war and addressed domestic and international concern about where Cold War nuclear rivalry might eventually lead without such restraint." Daryl G. Kimball, "Looking Back: The Nuclear Arms Control Legacy of Ronald Reagan," *ArmsControl.org*, accessed July 13, 2019, https://www.armscontrol.org/act/2004_07-08/Reagan.

fully use them; who rejoice in being persecuted, for they know that the powers have always persecuted those who bear witness to the steadfast love of God; who speak the truth, take no oaths or pledges, and forgive as they have been forgiven. Blessed are the peacemakers, proclaimed Jesus's beatitudes, those who are merciful, mournful, and poor in spirit.

But for Reagan's bastardized hope, it was America wielding nuclear intercontinental ballistic missiles—ironically called Peacekeepers—that would yield the end of history.

Clearly for Reagan history is not one damn meaningless thing after another. He refuses to spiritualize away the rhetoric of the New Testament. But he fundamentally changes the narrative. It is not the work of God in Christ evoking the end of history; it is not the people of God bearing humble, even suffering, witness to the work of God in Christ. Reagan has not merely redacted the story; he has changed the story. It is America, both agent of and witness to, the hope of the world.

Reagan, in other words, simply overlooks the fact that a nation-state cannot be the father of eschatological hope, because no nation-state can be legitimately wed to the kingdom of God. A dog cannot breed with a cat. Nor can the nation-state bear legitimate offspring with the kingdom of God. In fact, John's Apocalypse employs some of the most graphic sexual language in the New Testament on precisely this point. To those who seem tempted to enjoy a "friends with benefits" intimacy with the empire, John says: "come ye out of her," an apparent allusion to *coitus interruptus*. Before you climax, pull out.

In summary, Reagan casts a theological vision, describes the end of history, but casts the United States of America as the protagonist. In doing so, Reagan subverts the radical political purposes for which Jesus, Paul, and John employed such a vision. For them the kingdom of God transcends any and all human kingdoms, empires, and nation-states. Yet for Reagan the United States of America will carry human history to its destiny.

In response, many Christians contributed to the subversion of Christianity itself. In celebrating such political speech in service to a partisan agenda, they thereby celebrated the subversion of the nonpartisan agenda of Christianity. Pushed out on a limb, many Christians cheered on the one who took his sharp rhetorical saw to the branch.

Why would Christians sell their inheritance for a mess of American stew?

Perhaps one reason is this: they did not understand that Reagan—and the likes of Reagan—are liberals in sheep's clothing.

Liberalism

Christians must learn the differences between liberalism and Christianity. And the differences may not be what many presume.

Liberalism is a political theory and movement that focuses on the liberty of the individual over against various forms of authority or power. With the rise of the Enlightenment, old established forms of authority were challenged: that of the church, monarchies, and patriarchy. Much of the old was discounted, and the emphasis on the individual using his (and in time, her) autonomous reason and rationality was seen as the hallmark of the new. "Have the courage to use your own reason—that is the motto of the Enlightenment," said Immanuel Kant, one of the premier Enlightenment thinkers.[4]

There is much to celebrate about liberalism. Its movement allowed the undoing of a great deal of corrupt power-mongering, allowed for the redistribution of wealth held unjustly by powerful men, and challenged various forms of superstitious religious practice. In time, at its best, it would contribute to the undoing of slavery, the protection of children, and the (theoretical at least) equality of women, as well as (theoretically at least) racial equity. Various forms of scientific inquiry were set free in pursuit of truth, and many communities were given a degree of self-determination through democratic processes.

4. Immanuel Kant, *What Is Enlightenment?*, trans. and ed. L. W. Beck (Chicago: University of Chicago Press, 1955), 286.

Moreover, it can be and has been convincingly argued that Christian tradition contributed key philosophical resources needed in the rise of liberalism and democratic orders. (And one might make such a case without falling prey to the false notion, as argued below, that America is a so-called Christian nation.)

All these facets of Western liberalism should be celebrated. (And Christians have all manner of biblical and theological reasons to celebrate such: freedom of the press, for example, is analogous to Paul's insistence that everyone in the assembly should be allowed to have their say. And, it turns out, even with all of its challenges, that a free press provides a great check on corrupt power. For example, some sources report that no famine has ever grown in widespread destruction in countries where freedom of press reigns.)

Liberalism entails a number of institutional practices: democratic processes instead of patriarchal or monarchical hand-me-downs. Thomas Paine's *Common Sense* decried the idiocy of thinking that someone was capable of ruling well because he or she happened to be the heir of the current king or queen. Common sense, he insisted, would support the rejection of such medieval tradition and make space for liberalism. Thus, communities, nations, should be free to choose their own leaders, their own laws.

So, when small government advocates rail against the imposition of federal bureaucracy, they are being in this regard good liberals.

Liberalism makes similar moves with regard to economic institutions. Individuals should not be stuck in one economic class or station in life due to the traditions of their forebears. They should be allowed to choose their own vocation. They should be free—to use the language of the US founding documents—to enjoy their God-given rights to life, liberty, and the pursuit of happiness. For an Enlightenment thinker like John Locke, the pursuit of happiness entailed the pursuit of the accumulation of property, the potential amassing of wealth according to an individual's industry. Free-market capitalism, in other words, is liberalism made manifest in economic practice.

Liberalism makes similar moves with regard to religion. No one should impose on another individual a given religion. Individuals should be free to "worship at the church of their choice." There should be no state-established religion, for this would violate the conscience of individuals who should be free to pursue their own conception of God, the afterlife, or the responsibilities imposed on humankind by the Deity.

One of the fundamental philosophical *problems* with liberalism, from a Christian perspective, is this: liberalism does not explicitly concern itself with a shared conception of the meaning of life, the purpose of life, or the end of history. For a community as a whole to embrace the notion that "the glory of God is a human being fully alive" or to embrace the claim that the purpose of being human "is to glorify God, and enjoy God forever" would entail particular practices, habits, commitments, and convictions. As one example, for a community as a whole to embrace the notion that wealth must be employed for the common good and not wasted on extravagance or indulgence or vanity would entail yet another set of shared pursuits with attendant practices, habits, commitments, and convictions.

Classical liberalism does not concern itself with answering these sorts of questions. It is, instead, seeking to hold together some loose collective in which peoples of diverse ultimate commitments may abide together. Not only does it refuse to give a principled answer to these sorts of questions, but it in fact also rejects the notion that commonly shared answers to many such questions should be addressed in our shared public life. These matters are private. Thus individuals are free to make their own choices about the meaning of God or to choose their own values with regard to the disposal, use, and accumulation of wealth. But they must not expect that their convictions can in any way be made publicly relevant or important.

So, we might revise the contention here. Liberalism may in fact, after all, concern itself with the "meaning of life" or the "end of history," but only by *privatizing the question of what a good life entails*. Liberalism privatizes the good, but liberalism by definition refuses to make the question of "the good" a matter for rigorous public concern.

This does not mean, of course, that liberalism is unconcerned with ethics. A great number of ethical theories have proliferated since the rise of the Enlightenment, each trying to sort out what is right and what is wrong, with all manner of legalisms foisted on us. But these Enlightenment ethical theories differ sharply from many ancient moral traditions (as in the likes of Aristotle or Moses or the eighth-century BCE prophets or Jesus), all of which begin with the end in mind. These older moral traditions ask questions about what it means to be human, or they ask questions about where history is headed. Then, and only then, do they seek to describe the practices or morality or laws that should order common life, to fashion a people toward that end.

If you are unfamiliar with virtue traditions, you might think of it in simple terms such as this: What does it look like to be a good basketball player? Or an excellent musician? With an answer in mind, then determine what habits, dispositions, rules, and practices allow someone to become such? What habits, dispositions, and practices constitute such? This, with too much brevity, is a schema for the virtue traditions.

But liberalism does not think in such terms. One of the fundamental agendas of liberalism is *not* to determine any shared, thick conception of what the "good" entails. This is to be left to individuals. Individuals may choose to be basketball players or musicians or businesspersons or whatever, and they are free to do so.

That being said, however, liberalism needs some minimal morality by which it can be kept from self-destruction. After all, if all the individuals go mad pursuing their own privatized goods, then all hell will break loose. So, there must be *some* morality, some standards purportedly guaranteed by what liberalism calls rights.

Note then this contrast between the morality of liberalism and the morality of virtue traditions. In the virtue traditions, virtues are practices that make possible an excellence, a joy; they are a means of liberty. The violinist, for example, who has submitted to years of discipline, who has submitted painstakingly to good authority becomes free, thereby, to play and perform with a liberty otherwise not possible to the rest of us mere mortals. This was the vision of morality in days of old.

But with the advent of liberalism, morality and rights are primarily seen as a restriction of human liberty, not the pathway to greater freedom. Morality becomes, under the purview of liberalism, a *constraint* to human freedom.

By our own day the term *liberal* has come to be used for one branch of liberalism, while *conservative* is used for another branch of liberalism. One might summarize the similarities and differences between liberal liberals and conservative liberals this way: *they both support liberal institutions* such as constitutional democracy, maximizing individual liberties within certain parameters, the free exercise of religion within certain parameters, and the like. *But they disagree about the parameters.* They disagree about the places at which individual liberties should be limited.

Liberal liberals, for example, insist that a *maximum amount of freedom should be afforded* to an individual's use of their bodies, that a great deal of freedom should be extended with regard to sexual mores, gender identity, and sexual preference. For a liberal liberal, restrictions of abortion are, put most crassly, the federal government intruding into a woman's control over her own womb. But liberal liberals believe that the government *should limit* what individuals (and corporations) are allowed to do with their money and their guns.

Conservative liberals, on the other hand, insist that a *maximum amount of freedom should be afforded* to individuals and corporations in the use of their money and their guns. For a conservative liberal, restrictions of gun ownership are, painted in broad strokes, the beginning of the slippery slope of the federal government becoming a totalitarian state. But conservative liberals believe the government *should limit* what individuals are allowed to do with their bodies and sexual mores.

Generally speaking, neither the liberal liberals nor the conservative liberals are posing a fundamental challenge to the basic institutions of Western liberalism. Instead, *they are arguing over the proper forms of liberalism*, which, again, does not have any sort of rigorous or compelling or thick account of what it means to be human. Democrats and Republicans or the Tea Partiers and the Green Party are not arguing about whether to return to other forms of governance.

A king telling a businessman how to run his business is as repulsive to the conservative liberal as a king telling a woman what she will do with her womb is to the liberal liberal. They are not having an argument about whether to overthrow or question the foundations of the classical liberal tradition. They are *not* having an extramural debate; it is an intramural debate. They are having a family argument. And, of course, there is nothing like watching a family argument.

A potentially fruitful practice for American Christians, then, when discussing the politics of the nation-state, is for us to change our labels. Perhaps rather than ever using the term *conservative* let us substitute *conservative liberal*, and instead of using the term *liberal* let us substitute *liberal liberal*.

This would force us to think in different categories. Rather than seeing one such partisan movement as being the Christian one, we are forced to realize that the Tea Partier and the Green Partier *are* in fact *not trying to sort out the best way to be Christian but how to be the best partisan of liberalism.*

In other words, one of the first great steps Christianity can make in the Western world today is to realize that when we get co-opted or triangulated into the American family argument, we have thereby failed to understand either classical political liberalism or Christianity.

(It is important to state here that the would-be Christian may be able rightly to celebrate particular aspects of the liberal tradition. The point here is not to suggest that it would be preferred for us to have a philosopher-king [though there are times when a philosopher-king might be preferable to a mad ruler selected by democratic processes] or to have a socialist state. It all depends on the particulars. Instead, the point here is [a] to understand the differences between Christianity and liberalism, while [b] refusing to confuse the Christian eschatological vision with the American eschatological vision—which is to say that we must not bastardize Christian hope by seeking to bed American liberal might.)

To return to the sexual metaphor with which we began, when we reduce the political possibilities for the Christian church to being either a liberal liberal or a conservative liberal, we've bought hook, line, and sinker into the rhetoric that gives us a bastardized form of Christian hope.

It means we've been duped, been used, allowed ourselves to be used.

Christianity Is Neither
a Prostitute nor a Chaplain

SUMMARY

The American myth has used Christianity, and Christianity has too often been willingly used, has too often been a whore—to use the provocative and crass language of the Hebrew prophets. Or at best, Christianity has too often been a mere chaplain, blessing the imperialist exploits of the American empire.

As whore, the Christian community forsakes its covenant vow and shares the marriage bed with the powers that be in order to receive some sort of favor in return; the Christian church sells itself in order to share some measure of intimacy, some power, some access. Or as chaplain, Christianity reduces itself to mere spirituality, to some form of inner peace that has little to do with social or political realities; thus the most violent or unjust of deeds can be blessed with some bit of holiness, some prayer, some holy oil or sacrament.

EXPOSITION

When the American Civil War broke out in 1861, families and churches and campuses were split asunder, some men leaving home to fight for the Confederacy, some to fight for the Union. The campus of the University of Notre Dame was little different in this regard. Students left their alma mater and fought for both sides, which, of course, meant the very real possibility that classmate could slaughter classmate on the fields of battle.

Father William Corby, who would twice be the president of the university, left for the war as well. For three years he served as a chaplain for the Irish Brigade of the Union Army during the Civil War.

Corby was present in early July 1863 at Gettysburg. The opposing armies arrayed themselves opposite one another. Moved by the plight of the soldiers, Corby called together the regiment for what became a famed moment, memorialized in Paul Wood's dramatic painting *Absolution under Fire*. Knowing that many of them would shortly face their deaths, Corby assembled them to offer the prayer of absolution for their sins and blessed them in battle.

Some of the brigades had been called to arms. The battle was imminent. Colonel St. Clair Mulholland, attached to the Irish Brigade, gave this account:

> There is yet a few minutes to spare before starting, and the time is occupied in one of the most impressive religious ceremonies I have ever witnessed. . . . [The Irish Brigade] stood in columns of regiments closed in mass. As the large majority of its members were Catholics, the Chaplain of the brigade Rev. William Corby, CSC, proposed to give a general absolution to all the men before going into the fight. While this is customary in the armies of Catholic countries of Europe, it was perhaps the first time it was ever witnessed on this continent. . . . Father Corby stood upon a large rock in front of the brigade, addressing the men; he explained what he was about to do, saying that each one would receive the benefit of the absolution by making a sincere Act of Contrition, and firmly resolving to embrace the first opportunity of confessing his sins, urging them to do their duty well, and reminding them of the high and sacred nature of their trust as soldiers and the noble object for which they fought. The brigade was standing at "Order arms," and as he closed his address, every man fell on his knees, with head

bowed down. Then, stretching his right hand towards the brigade, Father Corby pronounced the words of absolution. The scene was more than impressive, it was awe-inspiring. Nearby, stood General Hancock, surrounded by a brilliant throng of officers, who had gathered to witness this very unusual occurrence and while there was profound silence in the ranks of the Second Corps, yet over to the left, out by the peach orchard and Little Round Top, where Weed, and Vincent, and Haslett were dying, the roar of the battle rose and swelled and reechoed through the woods. The act seemed to be in harmony with all the surroundings. I do not think there was a man in the brigade who did not offer up a heartfelt prayer. For some it was their last; they knelt there in their grave-clothes—in less than half an hour many of them were numbered with the dead of July 2.[1]

In such ways has the church often prostituted its graces, being used as mere chaplain to provide some awe, something heartfelt, some spirituality in the midst of the politics of the powers seeking to kill, steal, and destroy.

To be clear, the critique here is not of chaplains or chaplaincy as such, nor is the desire here to propagate any sort of moralistic employment of derogatory terms such as *whore*. With regard to *chaplain*, the question is whether the church has become what we might call a *mere chaplain to the state*, merely providing some so-called spiritual comfort to a state that has no interest in taking seriously the political shape of the gospel. Or put differently, *anyone who takes up the mantle of chaplain must ask whether one is a minister of the gospel or of the state.* Can one, will one, be able to bear witness to the specific counsel of the gospel regarding enemies, forgiveness, reconciliation, mercy, and the like, or is one simply expected to pronounce a blessing on whatever the powers that be determine shall be done?

1. St. C. Mulholland, *Notre Dame Scholastic* 13, no. 30 (April 3, 1880): 470–71, http://www.archives.nd.edu/Scholastic/VOL_0013/VOL_0013_ISSUE_0030 .pdf.

**Paul Wood, *Absolution under Fire,* 1891, depicting the famed scene
with Father Corby.** *The Snite Museum of Art, University of Notre Dame*

The question is whether the church will reduce itself to becoming a mere "court prophet," those so-called prophets who were
on the payroll of the king, divinizing for hire, speaking on behalf
of the divine, and always aware that the king had particular expec-
tations and agendas at work that the court prophet would ignore
to his peril. The true Hebrew prophets found these court prophets repugnant. The court prophets cried "peace!" when there was
no peace, and they tattled to the king when the visiting prophet
was denouncing greed and lust and injustice, and told the true
prophets to shut their mouths, go home, and show some respect
for the king. They would countenance no words of judgment on
the house of the king.

With regard to *whore* or *prostitute,* some feminist discourse
rightfully reminds us that such labels can be used as moralistic and
hegemonic mechanisms of the oppression of women. We must
be vigilant to avoid such ends. *Whore* clearly carries a connota-
tion of shame and judgment. But the judgment in the narrative of

the Hebrew Bible—say, for example, in the book of Hosea, which employs *whore* as the fundamental construct of its indictment of Israel—is concerned first not with sex. Moreover, it is certainly not intended as a mechanism of the degradation of women. It is, instead, first concerned with the breaking of covenant relationship. The sexual infidelity connoted in *whore* is but a consummate manifestation of the breaking of the marriage vow. It is a choice to violate a covenant and sacred vow. Consequently, our concern here is to ask how the church can renounce its whoring in forsaking its baptism. Our first concern must be with the church's possible renunciation of its pledge of first allegiance to the gospel, and whether the shape of the church's chaplaincy has become just one such manifestation of whoring.[2]

To return to Father Corby, many good souls will object, "The Union forces Father Corby blessed were seeking a good end, were fighting for a good cause!"

Here we begin to see the implications of the first three propositions.

1. Yes, justice for the oppressed matters because history matters. History is not merely one damn meaningless thing after another but an unfolding story in which the struggle for justice and liberty is central to the story line. History is an unfolding story of men and women grappling with courage and cowardice, seeking to give their lives in service to something larger than themselves, an awe-inspiring drama of the first order.

In contrast, it was often the slave masters and their allied clergy who reduced Christianity to a mere chaplain spirituality that could, with a straight face, tell slaves to obey their masters and wait for the sweet by-and-by when they could receive their heavenly reward. It was the Christian slave masters who refused to realize that history matters, that history is the stage upon which the justice of God is and shall be played out.

---

2. My thanks especially to Lauren White, Adam Boggess, and Phillip Camp for helping me nuance the claims here. Any insufficiency remaining is my own responsibility.

2. The abolitionists knew better than the spiritualizing slave masters that we are created for good and for God, and thus such creation entailed just and merciful human relations. They further rightly understood that the practices of slavery had to be undone. They knew that the ends toward which history is headed could break out *now* in the midst of the broken social condition in which they found themselves.

3. But then came a choice. On one hand this: to wed the Christian hope of liberty and justice to the nation-state's violence? Or on the other hand, this: to wed the Christian hope of liberty and justice to a proleptic stance in the world, in which Christians (a) would first do the hard work to abolish slavery among themselves, and then, or simultaneously, (b) call on their non-Christian neighbors to do the same and refuse to kill their unbelieving neighbor who has yet refused to accept the Christian practices of justice and mercy.

It is indispensable at this point to note that we Christians must not act as if various forms of oppression may be lightly looked over. Our call to take the way of Christ seriously must not be corrupted into *passivism*, into being passive in the face of violence or injustice. Instead, we are called to take up the way of Christ in response to violence and injustice. This is our political witness: to cheerfully love and serve and bear witness to the truth. We shall not take up the sword in the cause of the good because our God revealed in Christ did not do so. And this crucified Christ was vindicated in the resurrection, and this resurrection power is promised to those of us who are baptized into the way of Christ.

What if, for example, Father Corby had said to the assembled troops, many of them prepared to kill and be killed in service to the bastardized American-Christian hope, before the great battle:

> Friends, hear the word of the Lord: love your enemies; do good to those who despitefully use you; pray for those who hate you. This is your duty. Share your bread with the hungry. Put away your rifles, for our Lord has said that they who live by the sword will die by the sword. Put away your cannons, for the apostle said, "the weapons of our warfare are not carnal, but they are

mighty, through God, even to pull down strongholds." It is true that there is a great war waging in our land, in which some would reduce all things to economic concerns; in which some would reduce all to the rights of states; in which some would reduce all to their right to enslave their brothers or sisters and to tear apart their families without compassion or the most basic tenderness that holds together the tendrils of human community. We must not turn our backs on such a war lest the blood of our brothers and sisters cry out from the ground. But we are called to an even greater war in which the war is not against flesh and blood but against the strongholds of darkness, which can only be defeated by light and love and perseverance in the ways of the great God of heaven, revealed in this Jesus of Nazareth.

This is, of course, a real alternative for Christian political witness. Such a model, "neither right nor left nor religious," is substantively different from that of either the Christian progressive Left or the Christian traditional Right. And the witness of Christianity in the Western world may be utterly dependent on finding some such alternative.

Such an alternative for Christian reform has been raised at numerous junctures in Christian history. Leo Tolstoy, for example, in his satirical trouncing of the "triumph" of Christianity, mocked the manner in which the church welcomed Emperor Constantine into its ranks:

> No one said to him: "The kings exercise authority among the nations, but among you it shall be not so. Do not murder, do not commit adultery, do not lay up riches, judge not, condemn not, resist not him that is evil."
>
> But they said to him: "You wish to be called a Christian and to continue to be the chieftain of the robbers—to kill, burn, fight, lust, execute, and live in luxury? That can all be arranged."
>
> And they arranged a Christianity for him, and arranged it very smoothly, better even than could have been expected. They foresaw that, reading the Gospels, it might occur to him that

all this (*i.e.*, a Christian life) is demanded—and not the building of temples or worshiping in them. This they foresaw, and they carefully devised such a Christianity for him as would let him continue to live his old heathen life unembarrassed. On the one hand Christ, God's Son, only came to bring salvation to him and to everybody. Christ having died, Constantine can live as he likes. More even than that—one may repent and swallow a little bit of bread and some wine, and that will bring salvation, and all will be forgiven.

But more even than that: they sanctify his robber-chieftainship, and say that it proceeds from God, and they anoint him with holy oil. And he, on his side, arranges for them the congress of priests that they wish for, and orders them to say what each man's relation to God should be, and orders every one to repeat what they say.

And they all started repeating it, and were contented, and how this same religion has existed for fifteen hundred years, and other robber-chiefs have adopted it, and they have all been lubricated with holy oil, and they were all, all ordained by God. If any scoundrel robs every one and slays many people, they will oil him, and he will then be from God. In Russia, Catharine II, the adulteress who killed her husband, was from God; so, in France, was Napoleon. . . .

And as soon as one of the anointed robber-chiefs wishes his own and another folk to begin slaying each other, the priest[s] immediately prepare some holy water, sprinkle a cross (which Christ bore and on which he died because he repudiated such robbers), take the cross and bless the robber-chief in his work of slaughtering, hanging, and destroying.[3]

Tolstoy's sarcasm notwithstanding, he points us toward an alternative: that Christianity shall not be used by the powers that be to

---

3. Leo Tolstoy, "Church and State," trans. Aylmer Maude, in *Tolstoy's Writings on Civil Disobedience and Non-Violence* (New York: Bergman Publishers, 1967), 277–79.

bless their exploits. Christianity may and often will find particular areas of common ground with powers that be of left or right; Christianity may and often should serve in whatever legitimate ways the powers that be ask of its ranks; Christianity should and shall celebrate particular instances of justice and righteousness being done in the public square.

But Christianity shall not bless the ways of empire, of the nation-state, or of kings or prime ministers or presidents as they march off to take up the ways of destroying or slaughtering or lusting or burning or fighting or living in luxury while others live in deep need. Christianity shall no longer be used. It shall first focus on itself and its calls for repentance and call its own to the ways of Christ.

Christianity shall not prostitute itself by worshiping the flag, pledging allegiance, or singing the glories of the nation's wars. It shall not reduce itself to a chaplain dispensing pious pablum to ease the conscience, to give divine sanction to the very deeds and practices that the God revealed in Christ has condemned.[4]

But Christianity shall be an even better citizen: because it does not worship the flag or pledge its allegiance, and because it instead pledges in its baptism to a transnational community of reconciliation, forgiveness, and hospitality, which shall not be founded by sectarian oaths or accidental geographical boundaries.

Christianity shall not go to the White House to offer blessings before missile strikes. It shall not celebrate making the United States "great again" when such greatness connotes the very exercise of authority Jesus denounced as that of the "gentiles and sinners."

No, because Christianity has pledged allegiance to a proleptic life, it shall be a citizen more faithful than all the panoply of patriots: it shall be a citizen who speaks the truth persistently in love

---

4. For an example of such idolatry, see the two examples of First Baptist Dallas "Freedom Sunday," First Baptist Dallas, accessed July 15, 2019, http://freedomatfirstdallas.org and "20170529 Pastor Freedom Worship Digital Promo," *Vimeo*, accessed July 15, 2019, https://vimeo.com/272431309.

because it knows that lies and deceit are an acid which destroys the bonds of community. One who welcomes the stranger and the foreigner, for hospitality is the very character of God and thus is the grain of the universe. One who welcomes the gifts of life and children and the challenges of keeping one's vows, for it is in giving that we receive and in loving that we know the beauty of living.

It will be neither prostitute nor chaplain but a witness, a voice crying in the wilderness to "let justice roll down like waters, and righteousness like an overflowing stream"; a people, embodying an alternative politic in the world, neither Republican nor Democrat, but radically conservative and outrageously liberal; a servant, helping all, even, when possible, the principalities and powers to fulfill their created purpose of serving, not enslaving, not slaughtering, humankind.

And to be such a people, Christianity must know too that God alone is the hope of the world. And this is to say, of course, that the United States is not.

The United States Is Not
the Hope of the World

SUMMARY

If history is the scene of the unfolding of the good will of God, in which all wrongs shall be made right, and if this consummate hope of setting all things to rights has begun in the death, burial, and resurrection of Christ, then to wed this hope to America—indeed to any nation-state—is to bastardize the hope. And if the church of God's people in America is not to further propagate such a bastardized hope, then it must be neither prostitute nor chaplain. But more, the church must tell the truth and make clear the implications of the gospel: that the United States of America, even with all of its beauties, is not the hope of the world.

EXPOSITION

In his First Inaugural Address of 1801, Thomas Jefferson referred to the United States as the "the world's best hope." Abraham Lincoln, in his 1862 report on the state of the union, called the preservation of the union of the United States through the Civil War "the last best hope of earth." Woodrow Wilson would see the United States entry into World War I as vitally important for the unfolding of human history, and in naive, idealistic anticipation of the biblical hope, insisted that the war would be the "war to end all wars."

More pointedly, following the war, Wilson repeatedly said America would "save the world."[1]

> I have lived to see a day in which, after saturating myself most of my life in the history and traditions of America, I seem suddenly to see the culmination of American hope and history—all the orators seeing their dreams realized, if their spirits are looking on; all the men who spoke the noblest sentiments of America heartened with the sight of a great Nation responding to and acting upon those dreams, and saying, "At last, the world knows America as the savior of the world!"[2]

And in his 2019 State of the Union address, President Donald Trump insisted, "We must keep America first in our hearts. We must keep freedom alive in our souls. And we must always keep

---

1. On Wilson saying "save the world": he uses this phrase with regard to America in a number of speeches following World War I. *Addresses of President Wilson: Addresses Delivered by President Wilson on His Western Tour, September 4 to September 25, 1919 . . . etc.* (Washington, DC: Government Printing Office, 1919). "America, if I may say it without offense to great peoples for whom I have a profound admiration on the other side of the water, is the only national idealistic force in the world, and idealism is going to save the world" (147); "America—the constructive force in the world, the people who have done the most advanced thinking in the world, and the people who, God helping them, will lead and save the world" (174); he explicitly ties together the social function of hope, America, and the salvific nature of hope in America as well: "Throughout America you have got a conducting medium. You do not put forth an American idea and find it halted by this man or that or the other . . . but it spreads, it spreads by the natural contact of similar ideas and similar ambitions and similar hopes. For my fellow citizens, the only thing that lifts the world is hope. The only thing that can save the world is such arrangements as will convince the world that hope is not altogether without foundation" (205). A digitized version of the book is available at https://archive.org/details/addressesofpresi00wilsuoft.

   Similarly, see Woodrow Wilson, *The Hope of the World: Messages and Addresses* [. . .] (New York: Harper & Brothers, 1920), another collection of speeches made following WWI in which the theme of the "hope of the world" plays repeatedly.

2. *Addresses of President Wilson*, 206.

faith in America's destiny—that one Nation, under God, must be the hope and the promise and the light and the glory among all the nations of the world!"[3]

Alongside the Republican Lincoln, the Democrat Wilson, and the Republican Trump we can add all manner of others, such as the Democrat Beto O'Rourke in his recent announcement of his candidacy for president: "The only way for us to live up to the promise of America is to give it our all and to give it for all of us. We are truly now more than ever the last great hope of Earth."[4] Or as the Democrat secretary of state Madeleine Albright said, "If we have to use force, it is because we are America. We are the indispensable nation. We stand tall. We see further into the future."[5]

Against such messianic pretense, displayed by both the American Left and the American Right, our hearts must be schooled and steeled. We must insist that such logic betrays the gospel, for in employing such logic America has laid upon itself the mantle

3. "President Donald J. Trump's State of the Union Address," *Whitehouse.gov*, February 5, 2019, https://www.whitehouse.gov/briefings-statements/president-donald-j-trumps-state-union-address-2.

4. Beto O'Rourke, quoted in Brian Schwartz, "Beto O'Rourke Enters 2020 Presidential Race," CNBC, March 14, 2019, https://www.cnbc.com/2019/03/14/beto-orourke-enters-2020-presidential-race.html. My thanks to Tracy Hester for drawing my attention to this quote.

5. Madeline Albright, quoted in Bob Herbert, "In America; War Games," *New York Times*, February 22, 1998, https://www.nytimes.com/1998/02/22/opinion/in-america-war-games.html. My thanks to Rebecca Frazier for drawing this remarkable assertion to my attention. The State Department archive puts the language slightly differently, but the import is the same: "Let me say that we are doing everything possible so that American men and women in uniform do not have to go out there again. It is the threat of the use of force and our line-up there that is going to put force behind the diplomacy. But if we have to use force, it is because we are America; we are the indispensable nation. We stand tall and we see further than other countries into the future, and we see the danger here to all of us. I know that the American men and women in uniform are always prepared to sacrifice for freedom, democracy and the American way of life." Madeline Albright, interview by Matt Lauer, *Today Show*, February 19, 1998, https://1997-2001.state.gov/statements/1998/980219a.html.

of redemption, which is rightfully only laid upon, taken up by, the Holy Trinity.

"Hope" is first and foremost a *theological* category, and when such theological categories are exploited for the sake of the nation-state, hope has been bastardized.

We must not make such judgments out of hatred. We must root out condescension. There must be no "haters" among us. We must learn to love all that is beautiful and true and good about America and rightfully celebrate it all. Moreover, if we take seriously the prophetic voice as primarily an inside voice, and the kerygmatic voice as our outside voice, careful rhetorical judgment, careful strategic judgments must be made.

In any case, we must not reduce such observations to mere semantic arguments about a profligate use of the word *hope*. In any sort of nonultimate sense, *hope* may be an altogether helpful and appropriate term. We might rightly hope for peace among nations. We might rightly hope for the reduction of violence in our cities. We might rightly hope for the easing of partisan hostilities in our country. We might even rightfully hope that America might make global or domestic contributions to the reduction of hostilities or even to making durable peace in any given situation of conflict.

But when *hope* is used in an ultimate sense, it is a different matter. When we speak of the direction of history, the ultimate purpose of humankind, the meaning of life—when we speak of such ultimate concerns in terms of *hope*, we deny the most basic tenets of the gospel by claiming that the United States is the "last best hope of earth."

Returning again to Woodrow Wilson speaking a century ago following the "Great War" which was to be the "war to end all wars," he unashamedly ties together war making, redemption, America, and hope:

> Every mother knows that her pride in the son that she lost is due to the fact, not that he helped to beat Germany, but that he helped to save the world. It was that light the other people saw in the eyes of the boys that went over there, that light as of men

who see a distant horizon, that light as of men who have caught the gleam and inspiration of a great cause, and the armies of the United States seemed to those people on the other side of the sea like bodies of crusaders come out of a free nation to give freedom to their fellows, ready to sacrifice their lives for an idea, for an ideal, for the only thing that is worth living for, the spiritual purpose of redemption that rests in the hearts of mankind.[6]

Such high and noble rhetoric, we must learn to say again and again, is hope bastardized.

"In the 1940s, what could incite otherwise law-abiding white Christian Americans," asks Martin Marty, "to treat a group of fellow white Christian citizens like this?"

In Nebraska, one member of this group was castrated.
In Wyoming, another member was tarred and feathered.
In Maine, six members were reportedly beaten.
In Illinois, a caravan of group members was attacked.
In other states sheriffs looked the other way as people assaulted group members.
The group's meeting places were also attacked.
Members of the group were commonly arrested and then imprisoned without being charged.[7]

The offending group? The Jehovah's Witnesses. Their offense? They had circulated various pamphlets the likes of one titled *Rea-*

---

6. *Addresses of President Wilson*, 275.

7. Martin E. Marty, with Jonathan Moore, *Politics, Religion, and the Common Good* (San Francisco: Jossey-Bass, 2000), 23, quoted in William T. Cavanaugh, *The Myth of Religious Violence: Secular Ideology and the Roots of Modern Conflict* (New York: Oxford University Press, 2009), 181–82. Cavanaugh recounts this story and then notes: "One would think that the lesson Marty would draw from this story would be a warning against the violence of zealous nationalism. Astonishingly, the punch line of the story is a warning about the dangers of religion in public."

sons Why a True Follower of Jesus Christ Cannot Salute a Flag. The Supreme Court had ruled in 1940 that schoolchildren could be compelled to salute the flag. The Jehovah's Witnesses would have none of it. And so they received their measure of retaliatory violence.

This case highlights the fact that we are not here dealing with mere semantic arguments. We also are not dealing with matters of mere intellect. These are matters of *practice*, of formation—what we do and how we do it shape our appetites, our desires, and the pitter-patter of our hearts.

William Cavanaugh ironically notes that "ritually putting one's hand over one's heart and reciting a pledge of allegiance to a piece of cloth endowed with totemic powers" has been thought *not* to be a *religious* practice.[8] Neither Cavanaugh nor I am interested in necessarily making the case that the Pledge *is* a religious practice (simply because of the intellectual complexity in actually defining *religion*), though I find such a proposal fascinating. Here I am more interested in simply noting the ways in which oaths to the nation-state—and the sort of implicit hope entailed thereby, hope in the nation as savior—legitimate certain forms of violence (which is the task that Cavanaugh takes up at great length and in an immensely helpful way).

Because the United States has a policy of the nonestablishment of religion, we Christians in America have too often falsely assumed that the nation-state cannot be an idol. But idolatry is not merely an act of bowing down, of falsely making a self-conscious religious act of prostration or worship. Central to the practice of idolatry is giving ultimate status to some power that does not rightly wield such status. It is a practice that shapes our allegiance, our appetites, and our desires. It is a practice that engenders our sense of security, our sense of neighborliness, our sense of who our enemies are, and our sense of where to build walls and when to build them.

And the biblical witness exhibits on more than one occasion the sorts of consequences that come to those who challenge

8. Cavanaugh, *Myth of Religious Violence*, 182.

imperialist conceits. The tale of Shadrach, Meshach, and Abednego—their imperialist-given names—in the book of Daniel displays the social humiliation and threat of death heaped on those who will not bend the knee to the idolatrous empire. Even today the Jehovah's Witnesses—who refuse to pledge allegiance to any nation-state—have been designated an extremist group and are suffering arrest, prosecution, imprisonment, and in some cases torture in Russia.[9] And one wonders, what if Daniel's story had been told more steadfastly alongside the case of the Christian Colin Kaepernick, who sought to bear nonviolent witness to his own convictions? In what ways did an idolatrous nationalism engender the sort of visceral contempt evoked by the Christian Colin Kaepernick kneeling instead of standing—as Shadrach, Meshach, and Abednego had stood instead of kneeling?

With all this in mind, consider the US Capitol. When Abraham Lincoln was calling the United States the "last best hope of the earth," when Lincoln had insisted that the unity of the federation of states required a war that would kill 600,000, at just this time was the dome of the US Capitol being painted with the *Apotheosis of Washington*, a depiction of the founder of the nation-state among the gods.

Washington sits in the heavens, exalted among the gods and goddesses, himself becoming one of them, an apotheosis. It is clearly allegorical, but allegories matter. Allegories matter as much as the bedtime stories and fables we read our children matter. They are powerful forms of shaping both the personal and social psyche. They are powerful means of legitimating forms of social and political power.

There are significant academic subdisciplines that study the manner in which pagan storytelling legitimated certain sets of social relations and forms of social power. For example, the ancient

---

9. Marlo Safi, "Religious Persecution in Russia: A Jehovah's Witness on Trial," *National Review*, May 13, 2019, https://www.nationalreview.com/corner/religious-persecution-in-russia-a-jehovahs-witness-on-trial. And Scott Simon, "Opinion: Jehovah's Witnesses Cling to Faith Despite Arrests in Russia," *NPR*, February 23, 2019, https://www.npr.org/2019/02/23/697234127/opinion-jehovahs-witnesses-cling-to-faith-despite-arrests-in-russia.

Constantino Brumidi, *The Apotheosis of Washington,* **1865, fresco, US Capitol rotunda.** *HooverStreetStudios. Wikimedia Commons, CC-BY-NC 2.0*

Babylonian creation myth, by telling a tale of a violent and bloody creation of the universe in which humankind was created to serve the gods, legitimated the enslavement of the masses of the populace to serve the few powerful men who represented the gods.

If paganism does, in some such way, give divine sanction to social structures, give transcendent endorsement to the forays of the powerful, then perhaps the *Apotheosis of Washington* is more pagan than we might like to consider. We have Washington among the goddess Victoria, representing Victory, and the Goddess of Liberty. Arrayed between them are thirteen maidens, representing the original thirteen colonies, some with their backs to Washington, perhaps representing the rebelling colonies. Above Washington's head is this: *E Pluribus Unum.* This assertion of "out of many, one" served as one piece of the ideological justification for the civil war then under way.

For the apostle Paul, *E Pluribus Unum* was a consequence of the baptism of water and the Spirit into Christ; for Lincoln and the *Apotheosis of Washington, E Pluribus Unum* was a consequence of the baptism of blood and slaughter into the Union. Thus it is appropriate that directly beneath Washington is Columbia, goddess of war, with her raised sword and a shield that looks like an early model for Captain America's comic book shield, she trampling upon her enemies. The gods and goddesses of agriculture, science, commerce, mechanics, and the seas likewise are depicted, the various sources of American power, ingenuity, and accomplishment.

During this same era, of course, was the "Battle Hymn of the Republic" popularized, divinizing the military might of the federal forces. Note it is the "Battle *Hymn*." First published in 1862, the hymn originally, and throughout its patriotic history in the republic, has served as a public liturgical performance in which "the Lord" is made manifest in the fire and fury of the US military.[10] The rhetoric of the sacred, the affect of the melody and harmonies and climactic "Hallelujahs!" and the social and historical contexts of this liturgy all combine for a profound and moving formation of both the private and the public self: that America and its military triumphs are manifestation of the triumph of God in the world, a foretaste of the consummation of the end of history.

Within a few decades of the painting of Washington's *Apotheosis* and the publication of the "Battle Hymn," the senator and historian Albert Beveridge said this, speaking before the US Senate:

> God has not been preparing the English-speaking and Teutonic peoples for a thousand years for nothing but vain and idle self-contemplation and self-admiration. No! He made us master organizers of the world to establish system where chaos reigned.

10. "Battle Hymn of the Republic," *Atlantic Monthly* 9, no. 52 (February 1862):10, https://en.wikipedia.org/wiki/Battle_Hymn_of_the_Republic#/media /File:Battle_Hymn_of_the_Republic.jpg. My thanks to my colleague Robert Chandler for pointing me on numerous occasions to the manner in which such rhetoric of the sacred has operated in American discourse.

He has given us the spirit of progress to overwhelm the forces of reaction throughout the earth. He has made us adept in government that we may administer government among savage and senile peoples. Were it not for such a force as this the world would relapse into barbarism and night. And of all our race He has marked the American people as His chosen nation to finally lead in the regeneration of the world. This is the divine mission of America, and it holds for us all the profit, all the glory, all the happiness possible to man. We are trustees of the world's progress, guardians of its righteous peace. The judgment of the Master is upon us: "Ye have been faithful over a few things; I will make you rule over many things."[11]

Beveridge is insistent that the Constitution, in the doctrine of implied powers, "affirm[s] this essential and imperial power."[12] But more in our concern here is the continued manner in which Beveridge conflates his vision of American imperialist glory with the "divine mission," even employing the language of "great commission":

What shall history say of us? Shall it say that we renounced that holy trust, left the savage to his base condition, the wilderness to the reign of waste, deserted duty, abandoned glory, forget our sordid profit even? . . . Shall it say that, called by events to captain and command the proudest, ablest, purest race of history in history's noblest work, we declined that great commission? . . . No![13]

In Senator Beveridge's statement, says historian Ernest Lee Tuveson, "in capsule form are the elements of the idea I have called

11. Senator Albert Beveridge, "Policy regarding the Philippines," *U.S. Congressional Record—Senate*, January 9, 1900, 711, https://www.govinfo.gov/content/pkg/GPO-CRECB-1900-pt1-v33/pdf/GPO-CRECB-1900-pt1-v33.pdf.

12. Beveridge, "Policy regarding the Philippines."

13. Beveridge, "Policy regarding the Philippines."

'the redeemer nation.' Chosen race, chosen nation; millennial-utopia destiny for mankind; a continuing war between good (progress) and evil (reaction) in which the United States is to play a starring role as world redeemer."[14]

Let our would-be Christian eyes be opened to such idolatry and our prophetic voice set free to denounce it.

But some may ask, Where is the harm in such hopefulness? Is it not simple academic snobbery to pick at the use of the biblical visions in US political rhetoric?

At least three responses are important at this juncture. First, the harm is in the social propagation of falsehoods. It simply is not true that America is the hope of the world. Getting at the truth is always and undoubtedly a slippery and challenging matter. But to accept the cavalier use of language, the lax employment of lies, and the casual use of fake news, the careless use of theological constructs, we Christians must reconfigure one of our primary contributions to the world first as this: to speak the truth, to let our yes be yes, and our no be no. To say things as we see them without a shred of hatred in our hearts but always to speak truthfully. It simply is not true that America is the hope of the world.

Second, the harm is in the death and destruction. To take on messianic visions and wed these visions with imperial might and military force is to embrace a violent zeal against all those whom one counts as Canaanites, as those who are not us. If we are the chosen people, then others are not. The "other" then becomes the target of our violence and contempt. They become the legitimate targets seen in the dispossession of the people from this land, our fire-bombing of cities, our employment of torture, our dropping of the A-bomb, our harsh policies of exclusion.

Much scholarship has made clear, for example, the correlation between such messianic visions of American history and the genocide against Native Americans.[15] As the Europeans, newly come

14. Ernest Lee Tuveson, *Redeemer Nation: The Idea of America's Millennial Role* (Chicago: University of Chicago Press, 1968), vii–viii.
15. Two examples: Richard Drinnon, *Facing West: The Metaphysics of*

to the Americas, are to Israel, so the indigenous population are to the ancient Canaanites, and thus the Native Americans become the target of the genocidal wrath of the new Israel. (Thus in the US Capitol one also finds the momentous mural painted by Emanuel Leutze, *Westward the Course of Empire Takes Its Way*. Twenty by thirty feet in the House of Representatives, Leutze's vision, also painted in the opening years of the Civil War, depicts a valley of darkness and a valley of light, America and its explorers as agents realizing the manifest destiny of the westward expansion of the United States. Leutze and apparently the nineteenth-century US government had no problem with the use of the term *empire*, painted as it is on the walls of the Capitol itself.)

Third, the harm is in failing to comprehend the new possibilities made possible in the Christian vision and witness: the hope of the world is not dependent on any geographically bounded nation-state, not dependent on any king or prime minister or president, any congress or supreme court. It is dependent on a God who has revealed the ways of suffering love, vindicated in the resurrection, and now calling together a people not bounded by geographical boundaries, a people who will sow the seeds of such hope and possibility into the rich soil of human possibilities.

All this leads us to yet one more myth that must be rejected if would-be Christians in America would regain their political witness: the United States is not and never was a Christian nation.

The United States Was Not, Is Not, and Will Not Be a Christian Nation

SUMMARY

Even though we Christians in the West have too often allowed our faith to be spiritualized, such that it has no direct relevance to history, society, and politics, we've deeply known anyway that those things matter immensely. But having presupposed that the church and Christianity cannot be the first political home for our hope, we've gone rooting after other lovers. Thus hope—the theological assertion that history has a direction and a goal—has been bastardized in seeking to consummate a relationship between Christian hope and the powers that be. And at times the church has prostituted itself in seeking to bear some offspring between Christian hope and the powers that be.

There are some well-meaning but deluded souls who, because they believe in a bastardized hope, stake the political relevance of Christianity on the claim that the United States once was a Christian nation and that we must now work diligently to restore the Christian status of our nation. The tragic irony lies here: precisely those who think themselves agents for the good of Christianity in America are, in fact, subverting Christianity and doing immense harm. This claim that the United States was, is, or can be a Christian nation is (a) historically false, (b) theologically false, and (c) strategically alienating.

EXPOSITION

How could one not love the forests of Maine, the gorges of Tennessee's Cumberland plateau, the mesquite trees of West Texas, the ragged coastline of California—all of it like a hymn of praise, a song of thanksgiving for so much abundance and goodness? How could one not love the prophetic consciousness of Johnny Cash, the mesmerizing cadences of Don Williams, the angelic strains of Alison Krauss? Or considering sociopolitical greats, how could one not admire the virtues of industry and wit in Benjamin Franklin; the democratic impulses of the nineteenth-century social reformers; the cry for justice in the words of Frederick Douglass, Sojourner Truth, and Martin Luther King Jr.; the humility suffusing Abraham Lincoln's Second Inaugural Address; or the persistence and sheer human courage seen in the likes of the Wright Brothers, Thomas Edison, and Chuck Yeager—all like paeans to the human spirit?

But such love and affection must not be conflated with the myth of the Christian nation. To conflate love of country with the myth of a Christian nation is bad news, bad for the country and bad for Christianity. To claim that the United States once was a Christian nation, or to seek to recover some supposedly lost Christian nation status, is bad news because it is historically false, misunderstands basic Christian theology and practice, and contends for a strategy that is sure to backfire into resentment and hostility.

Historically False

Neither God nor Christianity is mentioned in the US Constitution. Religion is, of course, mentioned in the First Amendment, but the amendment requires freedom to practice religion as one chooses. And Article VI of the Constitution maintains that "No religious test shall ever be required as a qualification to any office or public trust under the United States."

There are references in the Declaration of Independence to

"Creator" and "Supreme Judge of the World." But these are phrases that any good deist could have and would have used.

The Treaty of Tripoli, ratified unanimously by the Congress in 1797 under the presidency of John Adams, maintained that "The government of the United States is not, in any sense, founded on the Christian religion."

Among the American Founding Fathers, such ambivalence— or in some cases antagonism to Christianity—is exhibited by Thomas Jefferson's correspondence with John Adams in 1823: "The truth is that the greatest enemies to the doctrines of Jesus are those calling themselves the expositors of them, who have perverted them for the structure of a system of fancy absolutely incomprehensible, and without any foundation in his genuine words."[1]

Jefferson's critical stance toward the doctrine of the virgin birth typifies much eighteenth-century suspicion toward so-called revealed religion:

> And the day will come when the mystical generation of Jesus, by the supreme being as his father in the womb of a virgin will be classed with the fable of the generation of Minerva in the brain of Jupiter. But we may hope that the dawn of reason and freedom of thought in these United States will do away all this artificial scaffolding, and restore to us the primitive and genuine doctrines of this the most venerated reformer of human errors.[2]

Like many eighteenth-century great minds, Jefferson saw value in the "moral teaching" of Jesus but rejected wholesale the theological narrative that birthed such teaching to the world. Jefferson's Bible—in which Jefferson, legend has it, took a penknife and cut out the parts of the Bible he found objectionable—ends

---

1. Cited in Paul Finkelman, ed., *Encyclopedia of American Civil Liberties*, vol. 1, A-F Index (New York: Routledge, 2006), 847.

2. Thomas Jefferson, "From Thomas Jefferson to John Adams, 11 April 1823," *Founders Online*, accessed July 16, 2019, https://founders.archives.gov /documents/Jefferson/98-01-02-3446.

5th CONGRESS.]   **No. 122.**   [1st SESSION.

TRIPOLI.

COMMUNICATED TO THE SENATE, MAY 26, 1797.

UNITED STATES, *May* 26, 1797.

Gentlemen of the Senate:

I lay before you, for your consideration and advice, a treaty of perpetual peace and friendship between the United States of America and the Bey and subjects of Tripoli, of Barbary, concluded, at Tripoli, on the 4th day of November, 1796.

JOHN ADAMS.

———

Treaty of peace and friendship between the United States of America and the Bey and Subjects of Tripoli, of Barbary.

ARTICLE 1. There is a firm and perpetual peace and friendship between the United States of America and the Bey and subjects of Tripoli, of Barbary, made by the free consent of both parties, and guarantied by the most potent Dey and Regency of Algiers.

ART. 2. If any goods belonging to any nation, with which either of the parties is at war, shall be loaded on board of vessels belonging to the other party, they shall pass free, and no attempt shall be made to take or detain them.

ART. 3. If any citizens, subjects, or effects, belonging to either party, shall be found on board a prize vessel, taken from an enemy by the other party, such citizens or subjects shall be set at liberty, and the effects restored to the owners.

ART. 4. Proper passports are to be given to all vessels of both parties, by which they are to be known. And considering the distance between the two countries, eighteen months, from the date of this treaty, shall be allowed for procuring such passports. During this interval the other papers, belonging to such vessels, shall be sufficient for their protection.

ART. 5. A citizen or subject of either party having bought a prize vessel, condemned by the other party, or by any other nation, the certificates of condemnation and bill of sale shall be a sufficient passport for such vessel for one year; this being a reasonable time for her to procure a proper passport.

ART. 6. Vessels of either party, putting into the ports of the other, and having need of provisions or other supplies, they shall be furnished at the market price. And if any such vessel shall so put in, from a disaster at sea, and have occasion to repair, she shall be at liberty to land and re-embark her cargo without paying any duties. But in no case shall she be compelled to land her cargo.

ART. 7. Should a vessel of either party be cast on the shore of the other. all proper assistance shall be given to her and her people; no pillage shall be allowed; the property shall remain at the disposition of the owners; and the crew protected and succored till they can be sent to their country.

ART. 8. If a vessel of either party should be attacked by an enemy, within gun-shot of the forts of the other, she shall be defended as much as possible. If she be in port she shall not be seized on, or attacked, when it is in the power of the other party to protect her. And when she proceeds to sea, no enemy shall be allowed to pursue her from the same port, within twenty-four hours after her departure.

ART. 9. The commerce between the United States and Tripoli; the protection to be given to merchants, masters of vessels, and seamen; the reciprocal right of establishing consuls in each country; and the privileges, immunities, and jurisdictions, to be enjoyed by such consuls, are declared to be on the same footing with those of the most favored nationsre spectively.

ART. 10. The money and presents demanded by the Bey of Tripoli, as a full and satisfactory consideration on his part, and on the part of his subjects, for this treaty of perpetual peace and friendship, are acknowledged to have been received by him previous to his signing the same, according to a receipt which is hereto annexed, except such part as is promised, on the part of the United States, to be delivered and paid by them on the arrival of their consul in Tripoli; of which part a note is likewise hereto annexed. And no pretence of any periodical tribute or further payments is ever to be made by either party.

ART. 11. As the Government of the United States of America is not, in any sense, founded on the Christian religion; as it has in itself no character of enmity against the laws, religion, or tranquillity, of Mussulmen; and, as the said States never entered into any war, or act of hostility against any Mahometan nation, it is declared by the parties, that no pretext, arrising from religious opinions, shall ever produce an interruption of the harmony existing between the two countries.

ART. 12. In case of any dispute, arising from a violation of any of the articles of this treaty, no appeal shall be made to arms; nor shall war be declared on any pretext whatever. But if the consul, residing at the place where the dispute shall happen, shall not be able to settle the same, an amicable reference shall be made to the mutual friend of the parties, the Dey of Algiers; the parties hereby engaging to abide by his decision. And he, by virtue of his signature to this treaty, engages for himself and successors to declare the justice of the case, according to the true interpretation of the treaty, and to use all the means in his power to enforce the observance of the same.

Signed and sealed at Tripoli, of Barbary, the 3d day of Junad, in the year of the Hegira 1211—corresponding with the 4th day of November, 1796, by

JUSSOF BASHAW MAHOMET, *Bey.*
MAMET, *Treasurer.*
AMET, *Minister of Marine.*
SOLIMAN KAYA.
GALEL, *General of the Troops.*
MAHOMET, *Commander of the City.*
AMET, *Chamberlain.*
ALLY, *Chief of the Divan.*
MAMET, *Secretary.*

Signed and sealed at Algiers, the 4th day of Argill, 1211—corresponding with the 3d day of January, 1797, by

HASSAN BASHAW, *Dey,*

And by the agent Plenipotentiary of the United States of America,

JOEL BARLOW.

The Treaty of Tripoli, 1797. *Library of Congress*

with Jesus of Nazareth having been crucified, placed in the tomb, and the stone rolled over the entrance. Jefferson is clearly not Christian in any orthodox sense, given such forthright denial of the resurrection of Jesus.

Or consider more recent language and developments. "In God We Trust" was first placed on coins in 1864, almost a century following the establishment of the country, and then only under significant political pressure. But we must look beneath mere words to the substance. It does not really matter whether any group of people says "in God we trust" or whether the citizenry pledges allegiance to one nation "under God." *The question is who the God is.* The question for would-be Christians is whether *God* carries sufficient specificity, content, to point us to the lordship of Christ.

With regard to the phrase "under God" as pertaining to the Pledge of Allegiance, it was a late addition. The original form of the Pledge did not have the words. But perhaps even more importantly, Francis Bellamy, the author of the original, intended the ritual nature of the repetition to have a formative role for schoolchildren: "it is the same way with the catechism, or the Lord's Prayer."[3]

Note too that the phrase "under God" was added in 1954, during the administration of President Eisenhower. And that same Eisenhower once noted, "our government has no sense unless it is founded in a deeply felt religious faith, and I don't care what it is."[4]

---

3. Francis Bellamy, quoted in William T. Cavanaugh, *The Myth of Religious Violence: Secular Ideology and the Roots of Modern Conflict* (New York: Oxford University Press, 2009), 117.

4. Dwight D. Eisenhower, quoted in Patrick Henry, "'And I Don't Care What It Is': The Tradition-History of a Civil Religion Proof-Text," *Journal of the American Academy of Religion* 49, no. 1 (March 23, 1981): 41. In his fascinating bit of investigative, text-critical work, Patrick Henry notes the many ways this citation from Eisenhower has been unfairly employed. The original context entails a conversation with a Soviet official in which Eisenhower was seeking to articulate a sort of religious tradition undergirding the American form of democracy, as opposed to the Bolshevist "religion" undergirding the Soviet's convictions. A fuller quotation is, "In other words, our form of government has no sense unless it is founded in a deeply felt religious faith, and I don't care what it is. With us of course it is the Judeo-Christian concept but it must be a religion that all men are

This leads us to our second point: Why the quest for a Christian America is problematic theologically.

Theologically False

America cannot possibly be a Christian nation because *no* nation-state can be a Christian nation-state. This is not a biased judgment about America. It is a simple matter of understanding what a nation-state is and what Christianity is. These two cannot be conjoined.

The following are some particulars.

- Nation-states are bounded geographically by borders. But the Christian church is *transnational* and is bounded by no artificial geographical boundaries.
- Nation-states are bounded procedurally by laws regarding citizenship. By and large, nation-states comprise those who are citizens according to arbitrary historical accident. Because I happened to have been born in Alabama, a former region of the Creek Nation but now a state of the United States of America, I am thus a citizen of the latter due to the two con-

---

created equal. So what was the use of me talking to Zuckov about that? Religion, he had been taught, was the opiate of the people." It is worth noting that this fuller context provides on the one hand a more helpful way of construing the contemporary conversation: those who (rightfully and in continuity with the argument I am making throughout this book) wish for our sociopolitical context to be engaged with and informed by the Christian tradition might indeed assert that our democratic traditions are informed by the Christian tradition. But they need not shoot themselves in the foot by overstating and overreaching by claiming that the United States once was, or must again be, a Christian nation. And yet Eisenhower's off-the-cuff comment here illustrates nonetheless a sort of theological carelessness that prioritizes the goods of the liberal democratic order—in this case, the need for some sort of theological conviction that could uphold equality and human rights—and makes secondary the sort of truth we Christians claim has been revealed in Jesus of Nazareth.

tingent facts of my birthplace and the time of my birth. The church, however, comprises those who are "members" following their own voluntary intentional commitment in baptism or confirmation. All are invited, and none are excluded.

- Nation-states build walls, literally or procedurally. The church of Christ welcomes all, literally and procedurally.

- Nation-states maintain their existence through military might and standing armies, precisely because they are geographically bounded.[5] The church, on the other hand, is an entity that lives by, lives according to, and bears witness to suffering love. The church does not depend on self-preservation. To make such a claim is not mere utopian theological assertion; it is a historical fact. All empires have fallen, and we have no reason to doubt that those in existence will not fall; meanwhile the Christian tradition has survived, for good or ill, through its own times of horrific failure and its times of creative faithfulness, for two millennia.

- Nation-states seek their own partisan agenda. This often takes the shape of developing alliances with other relatively like-minded nation-states. But in all cases it means at best a sort of relative cease-fire, or perhaps better, a negotiated form of mutual self-interest, and at worst it means war. But the Christian church's most fundamental calling—the "ministry of reconciliation"—means it must not ultimately identify itself

5. Peter Craigie, *The Problem of War in the Old Testament* (Grand Rapids: Eerdmans, 1979), makes the argument that the "problem of war in the Old Testament" must deal with precisely the issue that the nation of Israel, being geographically bounded, necessitated military force for its survival in the ancient world. Since God committed to a covenant people, and committed to those people in the midst of a world marred by violence and human rebellion, God likewise committed to the contingency of war. Craigie makes the claim, then—and I here I put it more crassly and pointedly than he—that the nation of Israel was, in effect, a failed experiment, and that in the Christian church we have a sort of People 2.0 that does not necessitate war for its survival because, among other things, it is not geographically bounded. See also now L. Daniel Hawk, *The Violence of the Biblical God* (Grand Rapids: Eerdmans, 2019).

with any given party, sect, nation-state, or other more narrow community of self-interest.

Given these sorts of mutually exclusive options, we must accept that *the quest for a Christian America betrays an elementary and fundamental misunderstanding of what Christianity is.* Those who piously assert the importance of a Christian America are precisely those, in other words, who are contributing to the very perversion of Christianity. They are not the friends of Christianity but perhaps its unknowing, unthinking, enemy. They may be wolves in sheep's clothing, and self-deluded wolves at that, who actually think themselves sheep.

Again it must be reiterated, to say such things is not, must not become, a Christian self-righteousness looking down its judgmental nose at America. (Again, the prophetic voice is our inside voice.) First, we Christians are called to love our neighbors. But, second, let us not forget that America has often had to school the church or at least school some particular parties of American Christians: breaking down patriarchy and racism are two of the most obvious examples. And for such externally imposed discipline we ought to be grateful.

The point here is simply a contention that a nation-state and the Christian faith are two very different things, and to seek to superimpose Christianity on the nation-state misunderstands Christianity or misunderstands nation-state or misunderstands both.

Some may insist that the critique here is too literal. They may insist that the rhetoric of "a Christian nation" is best taken loosely, as a way of saying "we support the greatest and historic values of America." Or perhaps even better, they may insist that the rhetoric of "a Christian nation" is simply shorthand for saying that our political traditions arose out of and in conversation with the Christian tradition.

If this is the case, then let the proponents of a Christian nation say what they mean. This will move us into more productive conversation. For it is undoubtedly true that one cannot make sense of American political traditions—the rhetoric, the institutions, the practices—without well understanding Christianity. Moreover, it would be shortsighted not to give appreciative recognition of the ways many of the relative political goods of the American system are indebted to Christian convictions and tradition.

But even such an improved conversation will raise other theological problems with the quest to ally America with Christianity. For example, notions of freedom in Western democracies are typically grounded in the notion of maximizing individualistic pursuits. Such freedom, generally speaking, is the liberty to do what one wants, within certain limits. But Christian notions of freedom entail the liberty, we might say, to do what one ought if one is to live a truly good and flourishing life. Freedom for the Christian is the capacity to live a truly good life. There is, in such ways, a wide and deep philosophical schism between the Western tradition and the Christian tradition. Thus to claim that "America is a Christian nation" is to be taken as a sort of sloppy claim that "we support the greatest and historic values of America" will not get us far.

Something similar can be said regarding the whole tradition of rights. While such language and institutions have served a terribly useful function in overthrowing various forms of oppression, and while the case can be made that the capacity of rights language to inhibit tyranny may in fact be indebted to Christian and Jewish convictions regarding human equality, such a political construct remains insufficiently construed, theologically speaking. For constitutional democracies life is a right. For Christians and Jews, life is a gift. Similarly, the very notion of a right to private property stands in tension with "all is gift."

And so forth. But these varied ways of claiming that America is a Christian nation—or that it was or that it can be—ultimately exhibit a deep theological insufficiency, if not outright failure.

Strategically Problematic

But not only is the quest for a Christian America problematic theologically. It is also problematic strategically:

If Christianity is, at best, being "salt and light" in the world,
as Jesus said;

if Christianity is, at best, a suffering love of all, including one's
enemies, as Jesus said;

if Christianity is, at best, a rejection of imposition and an embrace of generosity, as Jesus said;

if Christianity is grounded in the contention of Jesus to the
Pharisees and teachers of the law when he said, "go and
learn what this means: 'I desire mercy, not sacrifice'";

if these things be true, then the quest for a Christian America
can only be counted a strategic failure.

The early church grounded its strategy in its theology. One
could not embrace means and methods that opposed the theological convictions of the church. Means and method and theology had to be held together; indeed, they must still be held
together.

Thus, the early church, as illustrated by the anonymous "Letter
to Diognetus," which provides a beautiful depiction of early Christian life, says that God sent the Messiah to "bring salvation and
persuasion . . . , not to coerce—for God does not work through coercion."[6] Consequently, the early church rejected such compulsion.

This strategy question requires at least two observations.
First, our theology must inform our strategy, our tactics, our
methods for being a political alternative in the world. Second, a
more purely pragmatic consideration: that to adopt a strategy of
compulsion may in our own context simply backfire and do great
destruction. It is likely that we are now reaping the fruits of this
destruction in our own day; that in our quest to "save America"
we have turned away vast numbers of the youth of our land from
taking Christianity seriously; we have turned the way of Christ
into a laughingstock because those who say they believe it have
themselves rejected it.

---

6. "Epistle to Diognetus," ed. and trans. Bart D. Ehrman, in *The Apostolic
Fathers* (Cambridge: Harvard University Press, 2003), 145.

Again, then, the need for our inside prophetic voice to be raised, courageously and clearly. The Christian quest for a Christian America must be clearly rejected. We must find another way forward, another way of being salt and light, another way of living proleptically.

It is also crucial for us to acknowledge again the potential role *fear* may be playing: knowing that history matters, knowing that social and political goods matter, we grow fearful. "What will happen if America is not Christian?" But Christianity was birthed into human history as a minority report, and there is much abundance and many resources to live well and joyously without having to make others, as if we could, do the same. We may begin to see here that in the very attempt to make others do the same, we subvert our own attempts at being Christian.

It turns out, too, that the pursuit of Christian values may be just as damaging as the ill-conceived quest for a Christian America.

How Christian Values, and the Bible, Corrupt Christianity

SUMMARY

The Bible is itself a potential weapon of mass destruction, prone to use, abuse, and misuse. The idolatrous and blasphemous use of the Bible in contemporary politics is immensely destructive to Christianity. Hiding behind "the Bible says it," those who employ simplistic citations from the Bible in public discourse are often wrong and disingenuous. The notion of Christian values often works in a similar fashion: a loss of the overarching Christian narrative leads to a corruption of Christian witness.

EXPOSITION

The Bible says lots of things. It is a complex collection of writings from numerous and different cultural, historical, and social contexts. The Bible comprises numerous genres—poetry, history, legal codes, and more. But taken as a whole, the Bible is a narrative, or more, a *metanarrative*. That is, it is a holistic claim about the coming and going of human history, from top to bottom.

Given these realities, the Bible always requires interpretation, as does any document. One cannot pick and choose any one text and thereby pronounce "the Bible says it." (The US Constitution is not nearly so long and not nearly so removed in time or culture, and yet it requires extensive training in legal traditions to interpret it and apply it well. Even after extensive training, there remain ambiguity and argument.)

It may be true that the Bible says it, but this, by and large, taken alone, is an inconsequential observation. The Bible says that one ought not wear the likes of polyester (Lev. 19:19), that a man and woman committing adultery should both be put to death (Lev. 20:10), that if two men are in a fight and the wife of one of the men gets tangled up in the scuffle and grabs the genitals of the man her husband is fighting, then "you shall cut off her hand" (Deut. 25:11–12).

But given that the Bible is, on the whole, a narrative, it is insufficient to simply quote such texts without regard to the whole and without regard to cultural contexts, both the ancient and the contemporary. The Levitical teaching regarding the death penalty for adultery, for example, is certainly insufficient without reflection on John 8, in which the adulterous woman is cast before Jesus in an attempt to test him; without reflection on Jesus's encounter with the Samaritan woman at the well in John 4, herself having had five husbands and now living with yet another man to whom she was not married; without reflection on the meaning of Jesus's own crucifixion and its implications for capital punishment; and much more besides.

It is often the public Bible quoters who do such grave damage to Christian witness: the anti-intellectualism that sometimes parades under the banner of upholding the authority of Scripture contributes to the public mockery of Christian claims. Such literalism is, in fact, disrespectful with regard to the authority of Scripture. (It should be noted that it is not merely right-wing fundamentalists who represent such cavalier disregard; left-wing progressives can, with similar disdain, refuse to do the hard work of exegesis and hermeneutical inquiry, and dismiss the authority of Scripture due to their own sorts of literalist readings of the Bible.)

Consider the odd, to our ears, text from Deuteronomy 23:1: "No one whose testicles are crushed or whose penis is cut off shall be admitted to the assembly of the LORD." This prohibition—no one who is emasculated may participate in the "assembly of the

Lord"—is subsequently challenged. A later text envisions a coming day in which the eunuch will be welcomed into the house of the Lord and given "an everlasting name that shall not be cut off" (Isa. 56:5). Add to these first two plot points a third plot point following the resurrection and ascension of Christ, the poignant instance in which Philip is told by an angel to go to the road from Jerusalem going down toward Gaza. There he encounters a eunuch returning home to Ethiopia. This eunuch happened to be reading from the scroll of Isaiah in his chariot. Philip engages the man, teaches him, and within a brief time baptizes the eunuch: welcomed into the people of God (Acts 8).

This narrative arc illustrates the point well: unless each part is held within the whole, it can be misused, misappropriated, or maladapted.

A bit of chastisement from Augustine—himself dealing with those who were reading the book of Genesis in a way that brought disgrace to the church!—may be in order.

> Now, it is a disgraceful and dangerous thing for an infidel to hear a Christian, presumably giving the meaning of Holy Scripture, talking nonsense on these topics; and we should take all means to prevent such an embarrassing situation, in which people show up vast ignorance in a Christian and laugh it to scorn. The shame is not so much that an ignorant individual is derided, but that people outside the household of faith think our sacred writers held such opinions, and, to the great loss of those for whose salvation we toil, the writers of our Scripture are criticized and rejected as unlearned. . . .
>
> Reckless and incompetent expounders of Holy Scripture bring untold trouble and sorrow on their wiser brethren when they are caught in one of their mischievous false opinions and are taken to task by those who are not bound by the authority of our sacred books.[1]

---

1. Augustine, *The Literal Meaning of Genesis* 1.19.39, trans. John Hammond Taylor (New York: Newman Press, 1982), 42-43.

The point here is not to uphold a certain elitism in reading Scripture. Yet scriptural interpretation is not a matter that requires little training or formation.

The Problem of Redaction

Public Bible quoting in America is riddled, we might say, with the problem of redaction. Redaction—in which portions of a text are obscured or censored for the sake of legal concerns or for the sake of "safety and security"—may simply be a manner to change a story line altogether.

> This is how he said it, to which I strongly objected:
> "You are an ass! You should be ashamed of yourself!"

One possible redaction:

> This is how ▉▉▉▉▉▉▉▉▉▉▉▉▉ I strongly objected:
> "You are an ass! You should be ashamed of yourself!"

Such an egregious example of misrepresentation undoubtedly would be considered malicious.

A Christian values agenda may be just such an egregious instance of redaction: it cites particular commands, select proof texts, and yet drops key elements of the narrative.

We need not presume that those who are promulgating "Christian values" carry malicious intent. But it is crucial to understand that to whatever degree such rhetoric is selective, to that degree it is dangerous; the ignorance may not be willful, but it is not excusable.

We should also be wily enough to realize that Bible quoting may also be done with ill intent and in service to a narrow or partisan or oppressive agenda.

The Slave Bible

Consider the Slave Bible as one egregious and apparently malicious instance of Bible quoting. It is formally entitled *Parts of the Holy Bible, Selected for the Use of the Negro Slaves in the British West-India Islands.*[2] The 1807–1808 Slave Bible apparently sought to exclude texts that could incite rebellion and include texts that could foster obedience to masters—or such is one of the leading hypotheses regarding the provenance of the text.

If such a hypothesis be true, then the selection of texts was brilliant.

Included

is the account of the fall, and its consequences: "cursed is the ground for thy sake; in sorrow shalt thou eat of it all the days of thy life;

2. Michel Martin, "Slave Bible from the 1800s Omitted Key Passages That Could Incite Rebellion," *Weekend All Things Considered*, December 9, 2018, https://www.npr.org/2018/12/09/674995075/slave-bible-from-the -1800s-omitted-key-passages-that-could-incite-rebellion. See also Brandy Medders, "Fisk University Partners with the Museum of the Bible and the Smithsonian for Slave Bible Exhibition," Fisk University, December 3, 2018, https://www.fisk.edu/articles/fisk-university-partners-with-the-museum-of -the-bible-and-the-smithsonian-for-slave-bible-exhibition. In my assessment of what texts are included and excluded, here I am relying on David Charles Mills, *Unholy: The Slaves Bible* (np: Ghetto Kids, 2009), who duplicates the portions of the King James Version included in the redacted version and prints a "Comparative Table" showing what was included and what was excluded.

According to David Anthony Schmidt (personal correspondence, May 30, 2019), Senior Curator at the Museum of the Bible, there are currently two known editions or runs of the book (1807 and 1808). The copy currently on display in the Museum of the Bible in Washington, DC, is on loan from Fisk University and is from 1808: *Parts of the Holy Bible, Selected for the Use of the Negro Slaves in the British West-India Islands* (London: Law and Gilbert, 1808). A copy of the 1807 edition, which has only minor variations, is available online: *Select Parts of the Holy Bible for the Use of the Negro Slaves in the British West-India Islands* (London: Law and Gilbert, 1807), https://archive.org/details /selectpartsholyoounkngoog/page/n5.

Thorns also and thistles shall it bring forth to thee. . . . In the sweat of thy face shalt thou eat bread, till thou return unto the ground; for out of it wast thou taken: for dust thou art, and unto dust shalt thou return" (Gen. 3; all texts here taken from the KJV).

Excluded
is the call of Abram and the promise of redemption (Gen. 12)! No depiction of the longing for all things made new!

Included
is the enmity between Joseph and his brothers, the sale into slavery, and the day when "they brought Joseph into Egypt" (Gen. 37:28).

Excluded
is the deliverance from Egypt. (fully omitting Exod. 1–18).

Included
is the Lord blessing the house of Potiphar in which the faithful slave Joseph shows fidelity, the faithful slave Joseph who does not cast his eyes upon the master's wife, who, indeed, flees from the master's wife when she seeks to seduce him. Included is pharaoh as a deliverer in commissioning Joseph, saving the people through the power of the master.

Excluded
is the account of pharaoh as despot, as tyrant, as unmerciful slave master whose son is killed, whose army is thrown into the sea, whose power is undone. One finds no account of the harsh bondage or the imperialist policy of infanticide; one finds no account of Moses, who, growing weary of the harsh treatment of the Egyptian slave masters, kills one of the pitiless Egyptians and hides his body in the sand.

And one searches in vain for the great turning point in the narrative: "And it came to pass in process of time, that the king of Egypt died: and the children of Israel sighed by reason of the bondage, and they cried, and their cry came up unto God by reason of the bondage. And God heard their groaning, and God remembered his covenant with Abraham, with Isaac, and with Jacob" (Exod. 2:23–24).

And one searches in vain for Deuteronomy 15—to let debts be forgiven every seven years, slaves be freed every seven years; and for Leviticus 25, in which the landowners who have amassed great wealth redistribute the land to the original holders of the land.

There is no indictment from Amos of the wealthy, no mocking of the "cows of Bashan" with their great bowls of wine and their great summer houses and extensive estates, no denunciation from God such as this:

> I hate, I despise your festivals,
> and I take no delight in your solemn assemblies.
> Even though you offer me your burnt offerings and grain
> offerings,
> I will not accept them;
> and the offerings of well-being of your fatted animals
> I will not look upon.
> Take away from me the noise of your songs;
> I will not listen to the melody of your harps.
> But let justice roll down like waters,
> and righteousness like an ever-flowing stream.
> (Amos 5:21–24 NRSV)

Consider these passages from the New Testament:

Included

is Ephesians 6: "Servants, be obedient to them that are your masters according to the flesh, with fear and trembling, in singleness of your heart, as unto Christ; Not with eye-service, as menpleasers; but as the servants of Christ, doing the will of God from the heart; With good will doing service, as to the Lord, and not to men: Knowing that whatsoever good thing any man doeth, the same shall he receive of the Lord, whether he be bond or free."

Excluded
is Ephesians 2, which tells of the mercies of God, that all is by gift, that the hostility has been broken down, that Christ is our peace who "hath made both one, and hath broken down the middle wall of partition between us; Having abolished in his flesh the enmity, even the law of commandments contained in ordinances; for to make in himself of twain one new man, so making peace; And that he might reconcile both unto God in one body by the cross, having slain the enmity thereby: And came and preached peace to you which were afar off, and to them that were nigh."

Included
is Galatians 5.

Excluded
is Galatians 3.

Included
is Romans 12–13.

Excluded
is Romans 1–11.

That the so-called Slave Bible should cite Romans 13—in which the church is counseled to obey the rulers and authorities—while failing to include the bulk of the truly revolutionary and subversive texts of the New Testament is akin to a recent episode with former US Attorney General Jeff Sessions in which Sessions defended a zero tolerance policy on the US southern border, suggested that his "church friends"—who were being critical of the practice of separating families and keeping children within chain-link cages— ought to read Romans 13. "I would cite you to the Apostle Paul and his clear and wise command in Romans 13, to obey the laws of

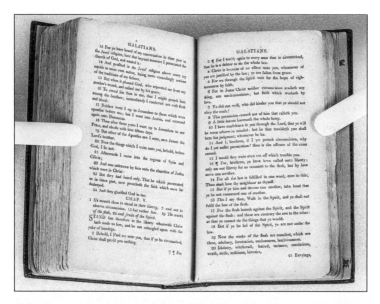

Galatians 1–5 (note the excision of Galatians chapters 2–4), in *Select Parts of the Holy Bible for the Use of the Negro Slaves in the British West-India Islands* (London: Law and Gilbert, 1807). *Fisk University, John Hope and Aurelia E. Franklin Library*

the government because God has ordained them for the purpose of order."[3]

Sessions's slick and clever counsel makes no mention of the very context of Romans 13. No mention of Romans 12:9–13: "Let love be genuine." "Love one another with mutual affection." "Be patient in suffering." And, especially pertinent, "extend hospitality to strangers." His employment of Romans 13 as a tool of

3. Jeff Sessions, "Attorney General Sessions Addresses Recent Criticisms of Zero Tolerance by Church Leaders," United States Department of Justice, June 14, 2018, https://www.justice.gov/opa/speech/attorney-general-sessions -addresses-recent-criticisms-zero-tolerance-church-leaders. See also "Jeff Sessions Is Not a Balaam's Ass," *Tokens*, June 20, 2018, https://www.tokensshow.com /blog/jeff-sessions-is-not-a-balaams-ass.

social conservatism makes the biblical citation become its own undoing. Paul's admonition to "obey the laws of the land" was not written as a weapon of social conservatism but was one element in a sort of subversively radical social liberalism that was convinced of the immense power of suffering love: it was a radical conservatism, a liberal orthodoxy, not a tool of right-wing political orthodoxies.

We must, in other words, learn to run any public and political employment of "the Bible says" through our redaction filters: *what is being ignored, left out, not told? What is being redacted?*

Consider yet one more public hullabaloo: Alabama Supreme Court justice Roy Moore and his installation of a five-thousand-pound block of marble with the Ten Commandments, exhibited with citations from the Declaration of Independence and the national anthem. By the redaction of the biblical context, we might say, Moore makes the Ten Commandments function in a way not originally intended. Nowhere is the narrative of Scripture exhibited: "I am the God who brought you out of Egypt . . ." Nowhere the radical social implications of such deliverance as seen in texts like Deuteronomy 15 or Leviticus 25. Instead, Moore makes the Ten Commandments function as an artifact of US sociopolitical conservatism and his redacted version of Christian values.

Roy Moore's original wooden plaque of the Ten Commandments was displayed behind his judge's bench in the Etowah County, Alabama, circuit court. And one wonders why the Ten Commandments and not the Sermon on the Mount? Why "Thou shalt not steal" and not "forgive us our debts as we forgive our debtors"? Why no "blessed are the merciful," no "judge not lest ye be judged," no "love your enemies and do good to those who despitefully use you"? Why no citation from the prophet Amos and his cries on behalf of the poor and the marginalized?

We would-be Christians must be keen to beware the bibliolatry, selective quoting, and Christian values that threaten to subvert Christianity itself. Just as the quest for a Christian America is no way forward, just as any sort of bastardized hope is no way forward, so is the Christian values agenda no way forward.

No one promised that a quest for a proleptic witness would be easy. And indeed there are yet a few more challenging truths to acknowledge that may prompt more fear.

But again: "do not be afraid."

Every Empire Falls

SUMMARY

Historical observation makes plain that all empires fall. More-over, throughout the biblical text there runs an anti-imperialist strand, pushing against the hubris and conceit of pharaoh, Baby-lon, Herod, and Rome. All their conceit finally fails them, and the systems of power of which they are both agents and pawns also fall, because no lord or authority or imperial might will stand against the triumph of the reign of God, in which all authority is handed over to the God and Creator of all things.

And to make such an observation is not a mere instance of *Schadenfreude*, an adolescent celebration at the misfortune of others. *To take seriously the manner in which empires fall allows would-be Christians to configure the correct target for their labors*: that the brilliance of our young need not be sacrificed to the strife of partisanship or to the military-industrial-congressional complex or to the dominance of global capitalism. To make such historical observations provides a more fruitful, nimble, and constructive ground from which to contribute to the good of the world.

EXPOSITION

The United States is an empire par excellence. It wields massive military force and economic power throughout the globe. Its military budget is not only more than that of any other country on the face of the planet, but its 2017 military budget was *larger than the next seven largest military budgets combined,* including China, Saudi Arabia, India, France, Russia, the United Kingdom, and Germany.[1] "Make America Great Again," within the context of such observations, sounds like the cry of an insecure imperialist. Insecure imperialists are highly dangerous and a threat to all manner of human goods.

Lord Acton is famed for having said that "power corrupts, and absolute power corrupts absolutely." While his assertion is problematic on numerous levels, this conventional wisdom serves as a sort of signpost pointing to the recurring historical fact that empires often become the victim of their own greed and grabbing. There are those, of course, who believe the United States may have already reached the point of no return, in that it has grabbed for too much and the chickens are coming home to roost.

Whether this is the case or not, it is important to note that to take such a long view of human history is neither pessimistic nor unpatriotic. Nor does it indicate a lack of love for one's country. It is simply a flat-footed realism that broadens the possibilities for construing the sociopolitical posture and possibilities of the Christian community.

Namely this: if (a) we recognize that Jesus explicitly rejected the so-called satanic imperialist shape for his kingdom, if (b) we recognize that the long history of the Christian church precedes the US empire, and if (c) we recognize that the Christian church shall extend well beyond the life cycle of the United States (for this is the very promise made to Peter by Jesus), then (d) we become free to be both judge and critic and contributor and citizen, knowing that the existence of the US empire is not our ultimate historical concern.

To be a truly conservative Christian, ironically, entails learning to do the same sort of sociopolitical critique that runs throughout

1. "U.S. Defense Spending Compared to Other Countries," Peter G. Peterson Foundation, May 3, 2019, https://www.pgpf.org/chart-archive/0053_defense-comparison.

Scripture. There is indeed an insistent critique of empire throughout the canon. In the Old Testament, pharaoh is the paradigmatic instance of arrogant imperialist might, finally reduced to nothing by the power of God and the indefatigable waves of history. Neither the hand of God nor the realpolitik of history will ignore the hubris of the mighty.

In some strange inversion of much ancient Christian and Jewish wisdom, critique of imperial might in our day has somehow been dubbed "liberal." But it is clearly *conservative* with regard to the authority of Scripture. And it is clearly conservative with regard to American politics, for part of the genius of the early American experiment was its critique and rejection of arbitrary, capricious employment of power. George Washington's counsel against standing armies and the Founding Fathers' insistence on three branches of government were commitments to such critiques of the hubris of power. To be truly conservative in an American sense is to realize the ways in which all may be tempted, all parties from right or left may fall prey to grasping after power in seeking to impose its imperialist way.

And to be authentically conservative in a Christian sense is to make nonpartisan critiques of empire, with equal opportunity criticism of the imperialism of either right or left. It is neither naive nor idealistic nor the province of the haters to critique fetishes with military might, nationalism, and American exceptionalism. It is instead historically savvy, politically conservative, and theologically conservative. It may be, for example, an exercise of deep love for country to say with all earnestness that all this running after imperial self-interest and yet more ICBMs and nuclear warheads and strategic submarines is an exercise unto death, and the faster one runs thus, the more quickly come the death pangs.[2]

The persistent biblical critique of imperialist might begins with the Genesis account itself and runs on throughout the canon

2. See the immensely helpful work of Andrew Bacevich on this score, e.g., his *The Limits of Power: The End of American Exceptionalism* (New York: Metropolitan Books, 2008).

to the closing pages of the New Testament. We might even say it is one of the cords of biblical revelation never far from the surface, which helps hold the whole account together.

The biblical creation account, according to many Hebrew Bible scholars, was juxtaposed in subversive ways against the imperialist Babylonian myth, in which the mighty justified their violence and subjugation of the masses. The Babylonian creation myth told of a universe created out of a bloody mess, a so-called "ontology of violence." The Babylonian mythology contended that the very nature of being was grounded in bloodshed and battle and war, that humans were created as a slave class to serve the victorious gods, and that the mighty—the priestly and the kingly class—imaged the gods, and thus the motley band of humans would need to serve the whims of the mighty.

Against such an imperialist ideology, the Genesis creation story depicted a so-called "ontology of peace," in which the universe was ordered by the loving word of God and humankind lovingly created for communion with God, and, moreover, humankind—all humankind—was made an image of this loving God's care and concern for all created things, good in themselves, indeed, very good.

With this sort of opening salvo against imperialist ideology, the cord runs on, page after page: *the tower of Babel*, a not-so-disguised critique of Babylonian pretense; *the call of Abraham*, called to leave his social and communal bonds that provided protection and plenty, and become a wanderer unto the call of God; *the boy Joseph*, unwittingly put in place by his envious brothers, to employ the power of empire for the good of the band of Hebrews, having been given the promise of God that they would be sustained by God's promise and generosity and not their own might; *the exodus from Egypt* following the pharaoh who knew not Joseph and treated the Hebrews with contempt, treated them like cogs in his imperial wheels, caring neither for their bodies nor their souls but only their productive output for his mighty endeavors.

Pharaoh had grown testy and knew full well how to employ the immense catalyzing force of cultural fear: if the Hebrews continue to grow in number in our midst, then we may be outnumbered; they may grow envious and start caring about justice and rise up against us in war. In an act of cultural defensiveness grounded in imperialist fear, pharaoh enacts a policy of infanticide. (Let us never be so naive as to think that empires will care about the babies of their enemies. The Spanish conquistadors bashed the heads of indigenous Central American babies, the German Nazis burned and gassed the children of the Jews, and the American military incinerated the Japanese babies of Tokyo, Hiroshima, and Nagasaki.)

It is worth pausing here to note that the battle with pharaoh, as depicted in the book of Exodus, is bloody and violent and apparently not even fair. (What does one do, for example, with the biblical contention that God "hardened Pharaoh's heart" on numerous occasions? And yet the text also notes, "And Pharaoh hardened his heart." In any case, the look-on-my-works-ye-Mighty-and-despair pharaoh found himself in a battle that he was in no manner going to win.) It is bloody and violent, and yet the very people pharaoh feared would rise up in violence against him are commanded by their God to sit tight, to be still, and to let God do what God was going to do.

The task of the Hebrews during the exodus was to fear and obey God, and *not* to fear and obey pharaoh. When the Hebrew midwives are ordered to kill Hebrew baby boys at birth, they simply refuse to do so. And when the imperial authorities inquire as to their disobedience, these wily women poke fun at the authorities: "oh my, well, you know these Hebrew women are vigorous, not like your Egyptian women; the labor pains hit them, they send for us midwives to come, and before we can get there, they've delivered their babies and are back up and out working for you all, meeting their brick quotas, and no chance for us to surreptitiously strangle those babies."

Thus pharaoh must up the ante. All right, then, when a Hebrew baby boy is born, you throw the child into the Nile. And it was by yet another wily act of resistance that the human deliverer of the Hebrews would find his way into the very halls of pharaoh's power. Little Moses is "thrown into the Nile," placed in a reed basket in the river, discovered by pharaoh's daughter, and at the resourceful wit of sister Miriam, Moses's mother gets put on the imperial payroll to nurse her own Hebrew baby boy, who would rise, in time, to call pharaoh to give an account that would lead to his great undoing and the deliverance of the Hebrews from their bondage.

One of the great ironies of the fall of the mighty: that which they inordinately fear often falls upon them. Their fears come upon them because of their own cowardice. Seeking to preempt that which they fear, they resort to injustice, violence, and oppression. Their focused energy brings the fear to life with a vigor and whirlwind perhaps not otherwise possible. Preemptive war is a privilege only of the mighty, a sowing of the wind to reap the whirlwind.

With the new life of Israel made possible, one great question in the unfolding narrative is whether Israel, with its hankering after having a king "like the nations," will be the alternative to Egypt intended in its founding. Certainly as depicted in the book of Deuteronomy, Israel was constituted as an alternative to the oppressive ways of Egypt. In Egypt there was an incessant demand for more productivity, economic growth, and labor output, but in Israel the people would rest every seven days, precisely, says Moses in Deuteronomy, because "you were slaves in Egypt." You *were* slaves in Egypt, but no longer. Put away the slave mentality and the social structures that make such a mentality possible. Instead, practice the liberating ways of this God who delivered you from such oppression. Learn to rest.

This very sabbath principle would be extrapolated into yet more economic and social practices: debts forgiven every seven years, the land allowed to lie fallow every seven years, indentured servants set free and given all they need to make their way in the world every seven years. In redemptive contrast to the ways of Egypt, the social and economic policies of the people of God were to embody a nonimperialist alternative.

Note that such distinctive social practices differ in marked ways from the policies of empire. Empires do not operate according to the ways of the God who delivers Hebrew slaves from the grasping hand of pharaoh. Empires do not forgive debt; they count on it. Empires, above all, are not willing to trust God to provide for their defense; they love accumulating to themselves vast might and power and glory.

Thus the biblical canon unfolds with continuing tales of kings thought mighty and empires thought impervious: Assyria with its bloodthirsty ways, whose king would set his throne before the gates of a newly conquered city, and there in his arrogant glory await his plunder, await his soldiers to pile up heads before him in a savage display of decapitation. Or the prophet Amos would denounce the brutality of the surrounding mighty nations: Damascus because "they have threshed Gilead with threshing sledges of iron" (Amos 1:3) or the Ammonites "because they have ripped open pregnant women in Gilead in order to enlarge their territory" (Amos 1:13).

In time the Babylonians would come stomping into Jerusalem, destroying the city, the walls, the temple, and carrying the people away into captivity, ruthless and merciless. And this tumultuous event—of being carried into exile—precipitated the great theological crisis of Israel's history. How could the God of deliverance allow Judah to be carried into captivity? How could the God who threw pharaoh and his chariots and horses and riders into their grave in the Red Sea permit the wicked Babylonians to rise against them?

The Babylonians knew full well the irony. Or at least the book of Psalms provides evidence that the Babylonians knew the irony:

By the rivers of Babylon—
    there we sat down and there we wept
    when we remembered Zion.
On the willows there
    we hung up our harps.
For there our captors
    asked us for songs,
and our tormentors asked for mirth, saying,
    "Sing us one of the songs of Zion!"
How could we sing the LORD's song
    in a foreign land? (Ps. 137:1–4)

Assyrian soldiers carry severed heads of their prisoners from the town of "-alammu," reign of Sennacherib, relief panel, 700–692 BC, from the Southwest Palace at Nineveh, British Museum, London. *Osama Shukir Muhammed Amin FRCP (Glasg). Wikimedia Commons, CC-BY-SA 4.0*

The mockery, the indignity, the violence of it all, and the utterly understandable fury that erupts:

> O daughter Babylon, you devastator!
>> Happy shall they be who pay you back
>> what you have done to us!
> Happy shall they be who take your little ones
>> and dash them against the rock! (vv. 8–9)

This horrific historical plunder of Israel—which continued even after the Persians allowed the people to return to Jerusalem—posed the great question of God's working in the world over against the strutting might of the bloody empires of the world. Would God allow God's people to continue to be dominated by the empires? Would the imperial word be the final word? Would the military might of the powerful determine the fate of human history or no?

By the time Jesus comes on the scene in first-century Palestine, there would have been many freedom fighters, numerous false messiahs, all seeking to undo the power of imperial might and kingly bloodletting, themselves often strung up to die and killed mercilessly. And when Herod the Great—that somewhat of a Jewish puppet-king of the Romans—hears from the wise men that a competing king had been born somewhere thereabouts, he plots to kill the newborn babe. But when his violence is foiled, he calls a play from pharaoh's playbook and kills all the little ones in and around Bethlehem.

It would be this empire, and all empires, to which Jesus's kingdom would be the great undoing. When Jesus went out preaching, he did not say, "Behold, I come declaring the true religion; embrace your personal relationship with me, and you shall enter heaven when you die." When Jesus went out preaching, he did not say, "Behold, I come declaring to you the means for you to know personal fulfillment and calm your existential angst." No, when Jesus went out preaching, he said, as the Synoptic Gospels summarize it: "Change! For God's kingdom is here."

Surely the truth revealed in Jesus does have a great deal to say to us about our personal communion with our Maker, and does have a great deal to say about our personal angst and struggles with our own mortality. But the declaration of the good news is summarized in the announcement of a new kingdom in which the bloodletting of history, the injustice of the nations, the brokenness of all manner of institutions, powers, and individual human lives are begun to be set right.

If we would be Christians, then, we must have faith to see the decline of empires—including those from which we may have derived many of our own benefits and power and personal privilege, often at the expense of others—as the inevitable consequence of the coming of God in Christ into the world. More, this does not even require Christian faith. This sort of realism about the manner in which might falls in upon itself is not a particularly novel observation, given that a simple historical survey indicates the inductively derived truth that all empires, in time, fall.

What is novel, of course, is the manner in which we are called to participate in the redemptive politics of the world. It is not through imperial might and military prowess but through the sort of servanthood and mercy exhibited in King Jesus. This is the great political fact to which all who follow Jesus must ultimately submit and thereby know a new and good life.

If the New Testament witness be true, it is the great political fact to which all human history will ultimately bend the knee and confess with the lips. And it invites us to the possibility of a nonpartisan contribution to the world in which we find ourselves, transcending the hostilities of left and right that shackle the imagination and political possibilities.

Christian Partisanship Is like
a Fistfight on the *Titanic*

SUMMARY

The previous chapter argued, from both a biblical and a historical perspective, that all empires have fallen and all empires shall, and that the coming of the kingdom of God is an alternative political fact that stands in tension with the empires, all of which are falling away.

If this is true, then the hostile and belligerent partisanship among American Christians might be compared to a fistfight over table manners on the sinking *Titanic*.

EXPOSITION

The fundamental identity of American Christians, if Christianity means anything, is in being Christian, not in being American. And the fundamental role of the Christianity community, to use the apostle's language, is to serve as a ministry of reconciliation, to serve as ministers of reconciliation to God and thereby to one another. To the degree that we fall prey to hysterics of partisanship, to that same degree have we lost our way as a Christian community.

Put differently, the partisan nature of Christianity in American politics is itself a denial of basic Christian political practices. This is true without even considering the *content* of the partisanship.

SOUTHERN CHIVALRY — ARGUMENT versus CLUB'S.

John L. Magee, *Southern Chivalry—Argument versus Club's*, **1856. A lithograph cartoon depicting Preston Brooks's attack on Charles Sumner in the US Senate chamber.** *Wikimedia Commons*

But in these days in which the partisanship of too many Christians takes on an increasingly militant nationalism, such partisanship is all the more devastating to Christian witness.

To be wildly partisan about presidential elections in the midst of the late days of an empire; to be ideologically hostile regarding small government versus big government; to be blindly belligerent regarding capitalism versus socialism, without keeping all these questions in their place of relative importance over against larger concerns; to cast aside all other concerns in favor of a government-mandated pro-life policy on the one hand versus a calloused rhetoric of pro-choice on the other—*all of this represents the failure of Christianity in America.*

This contention *does not lead to the conclusion that social policy is unimportant.* But it sets such policies, and the arguments over such policies, in a broader and relativizing context. (Again, I ask you patience. I shall explore in later chapters how Christians, convinced of the proposals presented in this manifesto, might think constructively and faithfully about social policy with regard to the unbelieving world.)

To reiterate, this proposition must not be construed as an excuse for withdrawal, for ignoring the serious issues and conversations that are, in fact, often occasioned by national politics. As has been stated repeatedly now, history *matters* to Christians, and the shape of institutions and social structures cannot be ignored because of some faux spirituality. Precisely because the Christian tradition has a rigorous vision of the end—the purpose, goal, consummation—of history, and precisely because of the political importance of the church of God in the world, two apparently self-contradictory but necessary conclusions follow:

- The politics of the world matters immensely—and consequently the metaphor of "table manners" is, at one level, inapt, if not offensive.
- But the politics of the world cannot, must not, claim our primary allegiance; the politics of the world must not be allowed to induce hostility among those who practice the politics of Jesus.

In other words, if we find ourselves wrought up in the hostility surrounding competing visions of liberalism, we must imagine different possibilities.

Following are two stories that may both illustrate the captivity of our imagination and point to some new possibilities.

First, a personal account. Some years ago I was asked to guest-preach at a large and prominent church. I had little time to prepare, just coming off some international travel, so I chose to use a sermon that I had recently published. It worked on paper; now I wanted to try it in public. The sermon seemed to fit the audience and context well, except for one illustration that I thought might stir up partisan frustration. In the published version I had taken to task a US senator who has never been shy about proclaiming his Christian identity and yet had recently spoken in a nationalistic, militaristic tone in a highly publicized speech. I decided to use an illustration that might fit the live sermon better and not unnecessarily stir up partisan reaction.

The international travel from which I had just returned was a survey trip to Santiago, Chile, preparing for a study-abroad semester with some undergrad students. The last museum my wife, Laura, and I had visited there was the Museum for Human Rights, in which the horrific tales of the coup of the dictator Pinochet were told, complete with detailed accounts of the manner and forms of torture and a vast wall covered with the pictures of the many who were "disappeared" by the powers that be in Chile.

It occurred to me early on that Sunday morning in preparation for the sermon that I did not know whether my three sons who would be in the audience that morning had ever heard a sermon in which a preacher made it clear that torture is morally repugnant and that Christians should by no means sit idly by when such horror is perpetuated. Moreover, a recent Pew study had found a correlation between higher church attendance, more conservative theological leanings, and a higher acceptance of torture as legitimate.[1]

So I proceeded that morning in my sermon on the Sermon on the Mount, undoubtedly my emotional and rhetorical levels elevated, my Alabama drawl in high relief, my preaching cadence employed: How can one be conservative, how can one claim to have a high view of the authority of Scripture, how can one read the Sermon on the Mount and support the practice of torture? And such like this did I ask from the pulpit.

I was taken by surprise by the anger that came at me following that sermon. Some members indicated that they wished to be informed should I ever preach in the church again so they could be sure not to be present. I was asked to meet with a select group of the leadership to discuss the fallout. On the third meeting I met

1. See "The Religious Dimensions of the Torture Debate," *Pew Research Center Religion & Public Life*, updated May 7, 2009, https://www.pewforum .org/2009/04/29/the-religious-dimensions-of-the-torture-debate; also see "The Torture Debate: A Closer Look," *Pew Research Center Religion & Public Life*, May 7, 2009, https://www.pewforum.org/2009/05/07/the-torture-debate-a -closer-look.

with one particular leader who told me he was so angry he couldn't look at me. We talked and argued.

He was angry that I seemed to be taking potshots at US political conservatives. I indicated that was not my first concern. If I had wanted to take on political conservatives, I told him, I could have cited another statistic from the study: the only group more likely to see torture as legitimate than American evangelicals who go to church often is Republicans.

"But," I went on, defending myself, "I did not mention Republicans. At that moment, I was much more concerned with those who see themselves as conservative Christians and yet support such policies. How"—I'm sure I droned on—"can you say you take seriously Jesus and support such?"

The most significant moment for me in that argument came in his next words, to this effect, "Oh. It never occurred to me that when you used the word *conservative* you meant 'theologically conservative.' I've just assumed that *theologically conservative* and *politically conservative* are the same thing."

That such an assumption would be possible in the Christian community says a great deal about the failure of Christianity in the Western world. I am *not* suggesting that it would have been better if this church leader had assumed simplistically that being theologically conservative entailed being a political liberal (or being a liberal liberal). I am suggesting that such an assumption illustrates the ways in which the Christian church has been taken captive by the American imagination, in such a way that the witness of Christianity has been obscured if not functionally obliterated.

If Christianity in America is to serve the good of the world, then it must imagine different possibilities.

A second, historical account illustrates that the partisan American Christian imagination of our day has not always been the prevailing one. It has not always been the case—even in recent history—that one party could somehow claim the vast swath of Christians who claim to take the orthodox claims of the gospel seriously. One of the great and overlooked cases of this is the infamous Scopes monkey trial in Dayton, Tennessee, in 1925.

Some facts of the case are fairly well known. The Butler Act, named after a farmer-legislator of the same name, had been passed by the state of Tennessee. It prohibited the teaching of the theory of evolution with regard to humankind in public schools.[2]

Soon enough a test case arose. A coach by the name of John Scopes was teaching biology and the theory of human evolution in Dayton. Soon charges were leveled. The case quickly took on national prominence. One of the greatest defense lawyers and orators of his day, an agnostic and social liberal named Clarence Darrow, agreed to defend Scopes and to do so without fee. On the other side, the public face of the prosecution was the widely celebrated William Jennings Bryan, yet another great orator of the day, a devout and conservative Christian, and—wait for it—a committed social liberal. Bryan had been three times Democratic Party candidate for US president, made strong anti-imperialist stances, and was a persistent advocate for workers and workers' rights. He was first nominated as the Democratic candidate for president in conjunction with the 1896 Democratic National Convention, after having delivered what is considered one of the greatest speeches in American history, "The Cross of Gold," in which Bryan decried the gold standard as an economic policy favoring the wealthy capitalist while ignoring the indispensable importance of the laborers and farmers. Following that speech there were some moments of silence, and then "bedlam broke loose, delirium reigned supreme," said the *Washington Post*, so great were his rhetorical powers, employed in behalf of workers.[3] He was a populist for the people, and he brought all that rhetorical power to bear in the Scopes trial.

A perhaps shocking note to some: Prior to the trial, young-earth creationism was not equated with conservative Christian

---

2. My storytelling here follows Ed Larson, *Summer for the Gods: The Scopes Trial and America's Continuing Debate over Science and Religion* (New York: Basic Books, 2006). See also Ed Larson et al., "The Tokens Show: Dayton," *TokensShow*, accessed July 17, 2019, www.TokensShow.com/dayton.

3. Richard Franklin Bensel, *Passion and Preferences: William Jennings Bryan and the 1896 Democratic National Convention* (Cambridge: Cambridge University Press, 2008), 233.

faith; even the editors of *The Fundamentals*, one of the leading literary sources of what became the American fundamentalist movement, thought it unnecessary to believe in a young earth. Many conservative Christian leaders—as was the case in England—had no problems accepting Darwin's theory of evolution, so long as some special status was held for the human species as bearers of the image of God.

What may be even more shocking are the reasons that Bryan believed the Darwinism debate to be socially significant. First, for Bryan, *ideological Darwinism was but militarism by another name.* The horrors of World War I, with its hitherto unknown industrialized killing, the slaughter of millions in the trenches of the European countryside with machines of war and its homicidal gases, were still a very recent memory. Such nationalistic war making was but "survival of the fittest" by another name. The world could not survive ideological acceptance of such a doctrine, feared Bryan; it was worth going to Dayton to make the case for the biblical vision of the goodness of God and the duty of humankind of love of neighbor, especially care for the weakest of our neighbors.

(It is worth noting that the textbook from which Mr. Scopes taught biology included a section on selective breeding for preferred characteristics in humans and had an explicit racist presumption.)

A second reason Bryan understood the Darwinism debate to be so important socially concerned the dangers of unfettered free-market capitalism: *the pursuit of profit without concern for neighbor or community or common good was also but "survival of the fittest" writ in economic terms.* For the very reason that Bryan's "Cross of Gold" speech had denounced the powerful elites in their version of trickle-down economics, he sought to denounce Darwinism because he saw it as legitimating, ideologically, the social assumption that would inevitably lead to oppression and subjugation of the masses at the hands of the "fittest."

Yet again, the point is not to argue the reader simplistically into a socially liberal viewpoint from the perspective of the political debates in the United States. (Much less is this narration intended to support any sort of young-earth creationism.) Instead, we would-be Christians must find new possibilities for fueling our social imagination. And in these stories we find two constructive possibilities for fueling such an alternative imagination. First, to acknowledge the ways in which our current partisanship has a history and has not always been the same as it is now. And second, to begin to fund an imagination in which we might ask ourselves what it may look like to first and foremost be Christians.

But this does not entail, again, any sociopolitical irrelevance of the powers that be, to which we must now turn.

Hostile Forces Have a Role
in the Unfolding of History

SUMMARY

Political realism insists that we must take things as they are and not as we may wish them to be and then work with those "facts on the ground." Such realism typically insists that competing interests of power must be balanced with other competing interests of power. In the history of Christian ethics, some Christian form of political realism has often insisted, therefore, that the nonviolence of Jesus is unrealistic if we are to make a difference or be relevant in the world.

We must both *accept* and *reject* the claims of the political realists. In fact, the Bible does exhibit a remarkable political realism and asserts that the powers that be have a significant sociopolitical role. And yet the New Testament simultaneously asserts that the church is called to a higher standard in its politic, namely, the way of Christ.

But this dualism does *not* mean that the church has nothing to say or that the church has nothing to contribute to the powers that be.

EXPOSITION

In the last half century, a great deal of biblical and theological work has sought to make sense of the pervasive New Testament language of power, thrones, dominions, authorities, and principalities.

Three brief notes on the characteristics of the powers: (1) They are "spiritual" in the sense that they cannot be reduced to mere materialistic phenomena or empirically observable data. The powers are such that agency is often ascribed to them, and in many cases, personal agency. (2) And yet they are sociological realities. They do not merely float in the ether, removed to some spiritual realm irrelevant to the historical. Thus particular historical characters are described as intimately intermingled with the various powers, even identified with the powers. The powers crucified Christ, says Paul in his first letter to the Corinthians; these historical characters who crucified Christ, or conspired in the crucifixion of Christ, were various first-century Jewish authorities in shocking alliance with various representatives of the Roman Empire. (3) But in spite of the second point, the book of Ephesians refuses to allow us to depict any particular person or persons as our enemy, but only the rebellious powers themselves. "For our struggle is not against enemies of blood and flesh, but against the rulers, against the authorities, against the cosmic powers of this present darkness, against the spiritual forces of evil in the heavenly places" (Eph. 6:12).

Add to these three characteristics four major additional observations about the powers in the New Testament, commonly noted by theologians who have sought to systematize such biblical teaching:

First, the powers were created for good. This is no surprise to any Christian or Jew who is familiar with the Genesis account, in which the recurring refrain of "it was good" structures the whole first chapter of that account. We may say it this way: we need economic structures, language, common moral norms, shared social commitments, and the like to have flourishing human communities.

Second, the powers often overreach. Created to serve humankind, they become, as Walter Wink puts it, "hellbent on control."[1] Intended to foster human flourishing, they become a mechanism

---

1. Walter Wink, *Engaging the Powers: Discernment and Resistance in a World of Domination* (Minneapolis: Augsburg Fortress, 1992), 49.

of oppression. The Bible is, we might say, the primordial tale of the Game of Thrones: always aware of the way in which there seems to be no depth to which the powers will not stoop to maintain, protect, and preserve their own. All that is good and beautiful gets coopted at best, corrupted at worst, into the ploys of the dominions.

Thus, the human practices made for good become corrupt and corrupting: "The sabbath was made for humankind, and not humankind for the sabbath," said Jesus (Mark 2:27). And yet by Jesus's day, Sabbath was a great power of overweening control and manipulation. Similarly, we might say, humankind was not made for markets, but markets for humankind; humankind was not made for sex, but sex for humankind; humankind was not made for land and country, but land and country made for humankind.

And yet markets become increasingly autonomous and care for little except to eat profits, caring not for the human resources consumed in the process. Sex becomes a vast cultural and industrial power, decimating homes and ruining souls, casting all aside in the wake of its titillation. Land and country become an idol demanding the blood sacrifice of its youth, refusing to allow respectful critics even to take a knee, but only and always with hand over heart, standing at attention.

The thrones and powers and dominions are discussed repeatedly in the New Testament. This fact is of great sociopolitical import and stands in great tension with the naiveté with which both stereotypical liberals and stereotypical conservatives often address social problems. It is they who often are the utopian idealists, not the writers of Scripture. The Bible is much more realistic about the challenges posed by broken social systems. Scripture has no naiveté about the ease with which such brokenness can be made right.

Modernists often act as if "sin" is an utterly unhelpful construct, but this is only because they do not understand the biblical concept. Sin is not some mere moralistic misstep; it not merely a willful breaking of an arbitrary, capricious rule handed down from the Deity-on-High. It is a fundamental missing the point, a fundamental transgression against beauty, truth, and goodness. It is a violation of the liberty of humankind and indeed the whole of creation. And such ventures in missing the point take on an immense power of destruction and can turn any good into a devastating wickedness. "Sin" becomes a slave-master. Because of this phenomenon of power, sin is on occasion personalized in the New Testament, its agency and willfulness subtle and baffling and powerful. The bonds of love for family, friends, and community, for example, may become the bondage of codependency and manipulative control on the personal end of the spectrum. This same sort of social bonding may become the bondage of nationalism and war at the social end of the spectrum.

The examples could be multiplied, but the basic, horrific dynamic remains constant: the good gifts of God, inordinately enjoyed, consumed, taken, all these throw upon us—as individuals, as communities, as civilizations—a mantle of oppression that is no simple matter to throw off.

This same sort of realism must characterize our own sharp social critique. The Bible is no utopian, do-gooder manifesto, but uncomfortably, sometimes painfully, realistic. Yet still the Bible depicts all powers—everything from king to priest, marketplace to temple, marriage bed to social policy—as potential gifts to human communities. Each gift may nonetheless oppress and overreach. Such realism must pervade our thinking regarding the relationship between church and world.

Third, even in their state of rebellion, the powers are used by God. The prophets insisted that the great superpowers of the ancient Near East were used by God in spite of their arrogance and injustice. Assyria, Babylon, Egypt, and Persia were all, at various points, depicted as agents for the sociopolitical agenda of God. That their mighty men were unaware made them no less the agents of God's purposes.

Similarly, the apostle Paul will insist that the powers, when they check violence and keep chaos at bay, are the servants of God. Paul insists that the first-century Christians should pray for the kings and authorities, that they may keep the peace, so the witness of the church may go forth unhindered by social turmoil.

Fourth, the powers—given that they are good creations of God—do not need to be destroyed but to be redeemed. Or, perhaps more accurately, the particular manifestations of the rebellious powers, claims the New Testament (see especially 1 Cor. 15), will in fact be destroyed. But the powers created for good shall be redeemed and rightly ordered toward the good of God's bountiful and beautiful creation.

There are at least two reasons Christians are not anarchists: first, since all power and dominion was created for good, to give glory to the Creator and serve the goods of the creation, we can and should celebrate when such power leans toward its intended functions. Such a posture takes seriously, then, that relative goods are important and should not be taken lightly. A relatively stable democracy with due process and shared constitutional commitments to the rule of law, even if full of bickering and brokenness, is undoubtedly preferable to a ruthless totalitarian dictatorship that tortures dissidents, silences critique, and ignores the plight of the poor and hungry.

Instead of hitching our wagon to any particular partisan horse, then, the Christian community is called to practice the sort of pragmatic realism embodied in Scripture itself.

A second reason that Christians are not anarchists is that we are acutely aware that destroying one partisan representative of oppressive power does not ensure the destruction of the power of death itself. Death has already been defeated. Death is suffering its own death pangs. To play the games of death only deepens the struggle. To put it differently, destroy "the Man," and there will be a line of willing characters to take on the role afresh.

Until the consummation of the kingdom of God—until death has been finally defeated and resurrection triumphant—there are no utopian possibilities to be had. Any given structure of power may be more or less in service to its created ends, but there is no idyllic or partisan utopian solution to be had.

This is key to understanding the fundamental social and political posture of the New Testament: the end of history has been inaugurated, but until its final consummation there are many who

Workshop of Sebastiaen Vrancx (1573–1647), *A Landscape with Travellers Ambushed Outside a Small Town,* **oil on panel.** *Sotheby's London, 24 April 2008, lot 20. Wikimedia Commons*

still live according to the ways of death. In the midst of this real and often perverse pursuit of the ways of death, the powers—even in their self-centered and perverse grappling after power—still serve a useful function, because the powers themselves often have something at stake in staving off chaos. A balance of powers can keep such chaos at bay. The Bible claims that God employs a balance of powers precisely in service to keeping wickedness in check.

Such biblical realism allows us to reject the naive and idealistic notion that evil can be destroyed through the likes of war. It is a self-mockery of American Christianity, and a public exhibition of biblical illiteracy, that President George W. Bush, a self-proclaimed Christian, insisted that he had begun a war to "defeat evil." The self-mockery was deepened in that so few Christians raised the slightest objection to such claims.

But what then is the New Testament's prescription for the people of God prior to the time of the consummation of the kingdom of God, vis-à-vis the powers that be? The New Testament says precious little on this score, or at least it says very little in a direct fashion. But we are given at least one direct counsel: the church should show to the powers the wisdom of God (Eph. 3; discussed in proposition 13).

The powers have their own wisdom—self-maintenance, "hell-bent on control." Again, as already noted, God in God's providence is still using the powers to check chaos (Rom. 13; 1 Tim. 2). But their wisdom is not the wisdom of God, revealed in the suffering servanthood of Christ. Thus the church is called to bear witness to the powers the public goods and sociopolitical relevance of the way of Christ.

This is key for would-be Christians. We go into the world wise as serpents, harmless as doves, wise in carrying with us an eyes-wide-open knowledge of the machinations of power but refusing to fall prey to the coercion and violence of those powers, and bearing witness to the good news of the strength and power of truth telling, generosity, justice, and mercy. We go into the world fully aware of the ways in which Karl Marx was right—that industrialization has alienated human beings from their work and one another—and fully aware of the ways in which Adam Smith was right—that social selfishness is a strong mechanism for the generation of material wealth; and knowing that any sort of ideological or utopian assertion of either Marx's or Smith's vision leads to death and destruction and endless war.

Smith and Marx may both have helpful things to teach us about the nature of humankind, the nature of historical struggles, or the nature of human appetites and the social mechanisms that arise out of those appetites. But so often overlooked are the ways in which the ideological capitalists and the ideological communists are precisely the same: committed to a utopian vision of the world, they employ violence and war to propagate their vision. Thus Marx ends his *Manifesto* calling for the "forcible overthrow of all existing social conditions," just as the twentieth-century capitalists waged all manner of war in Central and South America or Vietnam or the Korean Peninsula, seeking to make the world safe for capitalist expansion.

A Christian political manifesto must simultaneously be more realistic and more rigorous in its ethic. We must be more realistic in acknowledging the pervasive nature of fallen structures of power, which may be made manifest as much in socialist bureaucracies as in global capitalism, as much in Stalin's mass murder as in the West's wars in the Middle East. Simultaneously, we must be more rigorous, insisting what neither Milton Friedman nor Karl Marx will insist: that the good news of the kingdom of God has already triumphed over the forces of war and death and imposition, and that we too shall love and serve in the same ways as our Christ.

Of course there is much more to be said about how Christians may "show to the powers the wisdom of God." But, as will discussed below, this must be construed as an *ad hoc* sociopolitical witness, dealing with each issue, abuse, or injustice as it arises without assuming that the capitalists or communists, the Left or the Right, the conservatives or the progressives will necessarily have the answer.

More on Romans 13, with a Nod to Revelation 13

Due to the rhetorical significance of the apostle Paul's teaching in Romans 13, more commentary may be helpful here.[2]

To summarize matters already raised but that are indispensable for rightly construing Romans 13: The vocation of the church is to embody the peaceable way of the kingdom of God. This must be held alongside a realism about the ongoing reality of sin in the world. The church's vocation held alongside the church's realism then provides specification for *the vocation of the powers and governing authorities.* Given that the triumph over the power of sin is not yet final, we may expect that wickedness will still rear its ugly head, will strike and lash out. Corruption and murder and death

---

2. This section is adapted from portions of an essay originally published as "What about Romans 13: 'Let Every Soul Be Subject'?" in *A Faith Not Worth Fighting For: Addressing Commonly Asked Questions about Christian Nonviolence*, ed. Tripp York and Justin Bronson Barringer (Eugene, OR: Cascade Books, 2012). Used by permission. To download a free PDF of the full essay, visit http://www.leeccamp.com/romans13.

have not yet been finally defeated, and thus we continue to see its work made manifest on the pages of history. It is precisely this reality that defines the work of the governing authorities, which is to channel the vengeance and wickedness back upon itself, to limit the destructive and maddening effects of violence by turning it in on itself.

As we have seen, the vocation of the church is to embody the new. But all have not received the new as good news, and thus they continue to live under bondage to the forces of death. What then? The governing authorities are ordered by God to have a preservative effect. Unlike Luther, who claimed that the governing authorities were part of the "orders of creation," Dietrich Bonhoeffer called the powers "orders of preservation." That is, they have a function of employing a sharply limited amount of violence or coercion in service to checking chaos, keeping madness at bay. As the prince or king or emperor may thus excusably employ coercion in this manner, meanwhile the church embodies the new and proclaims the new, inviting all to come to participate in the new.

Some have suggested it is important to make a distinction between *ordaining* and *ordering*—that Romans 13 claims that God has ordered the powers but not ordained any particular power, has not specifically approved the behavior of what any particular government does. Instead, in God's providence, they are brought into God's ordering of human history.

Thus, with little systematic consideration, the New Testament writers simply assume a given role for the governing authorities that may be summarized thus: the governing authorities, with their police function, serve the larger mission of the church. In parallel with Romans 13, 1 Timothy 2, and 1 Peter 2, all depict the relationship between church and governing authorities in this way.

This stands in continuity with the Old Testament witness, in which the powers of the world were used in God's sovereignty for God's purposes in history, as noted previously. Assyria, Babylon, Egypt, and Persia are all described in various ways as being the servants of God's purposes, typically employed for punishing and chastising the wicked. These (themselves often wicked) nations are God's "ministers" in the limited sense of serving God's overarching order, in that God employs the arrogance and violence of the nations against one another so that the earth and its creatures are not utterly destroyed.

Several notes in this regard.

First, this way of putting the matter stands at odds with the assumptions already discussed at the heart of Western, liberal democratic orders: of a privatized so-called religion, in which this religion, as a compartmentalizable element of life, need not, and for many ought not, impinge on the so-called realm of the public. For some secularists, religion is simply dispensable and unnecessary altogether, though notions of human rights are thought to require a political order in which so-called religion is protected as a so-called private affair. For others, religion turns out to be something that is needed by democratic regimes, providing something like a moral compass or ethical ballast to a ship that would otherwise wander aimlessly. In this view, called an "instrumental view of the church," the church serves the broader and purportedly more public role of the nation-state. The nation-state, or democracy, is seen as the larger, more public, and more significant player in human history. So far as history is concerned, the nation-state is seen as the *historical savior*, is seen as the "last great hope of the earth." The church thus serves democracy and not the other way around.

Thus the New Testament claim is, from the start, offensive to modern sensibilities. In the New Testament it is the governing authorities who serve the church rather than the other way around. Ephesians 3 notes, for example, that the salvific wisdom of God is revealed to the powers *in the church*. "Although I am the very least of all the saints, this grace was given to me to bring to the Gentiles the news of the boundless riches of Christ, and to make everyone see what is the plan of the mystery hidden for ages in God who created all things; so that through the church the wisdom of God in its rich variety might now be made known to the rulers and authorities in the heavenly places" (Eph. 3:8–10).

Paul's decidedly anti-modern stance in 1 Corinthians 2:8 further demonstrates this claim. When believers go before unbelievers to settle disputes among themselves, Paul can hardly fathom it. Why, he asks, would you take a dispute to be judged by unbelievers when it is the believers who will, in the end, judge the world? It would be better to be defrauded, he claims.[3]

It has been suggested by others that it is almost as if the apostle Paul depicts the scenario this way: the church is putting on the stage show, while the governing authorities serve as the ushers at the show. The usher is necessary and helpful. But the artists and musicians and performers are the reason for the gathering. And it does not serve the affair at all for the artists and musicians and performers to busy themselves with ushering, for then the show cannot go on. They have a special vocation to which they must attend. From the New Testament perspective, the state and governing authorities serve the mission of the church, and the church is the primary character in God's mission to the world. This claim must not and cannot be construed in a triumphalist manner, in which the church then seeks to arrogantly vaunt itself over the powers and over the peoples: for the vocation and mission of the church is to embody suffering love and the peace of God's kingdom, and call all to participate in this reign.

Second, for the Christian to "be subject" to the authorities cannot mean, then, "blind subjection."[4] There *is* a certain social conservatism in the text on this score: the powers that be are ordered by God to serve their role of keeping wickedness at bay through the employment of a limited coercive force. In serving that role, Christians must not seek to overthrow governments but should acknowledge the ordination or vocation of those powers. (It is no small irony that Romans 13 is often employed to counsel a sort of sociopolitical conservatism—"obey the au-

---

3. Oscar Cullmann, "Paul and the State," in *The State in the New Testament* (New York: Scribner's, 1956), 56.

4. Karl Barth, *A Shorter Commentary on Romans*, trans. Chr. Kaiser Verlag (London: SCM Press, 1959), 157–58.

thorities!"—but that the implications are never explored on Independence Day.)

But again, this cannot mean a blind subjection, an indiscriminate blessing of whatever the powers do. Such a position would obviously stand at odds with the overarching teaching of the entire Bible. From the prophet Nathan to the exiled Daniel, from John the Baptizer to Peter the apostle, a consistent prioritization of allegiances appears. "We must obey God rather than human authorities." To the degree that the human authority requires something of us which does not stand at odds with our first and prior allegiance to Jesus as Lord, to that same degree must we yield our obedience. There is *something* that we must yield to Caesar, but only when whatever Caesar demands has not been previously demanded by the Creator.[5]

Third, then, the powers may become demonic, may begin to demand for themselves absolute and abject obedience. The powers may begin to assert themselves as a god. Instead of serving the very limited role ordained by God, the powers too often see themselves as saviors, as being the hope and light of the world. And this terribly dangerous conceit is not a dynamic with which the New Testament is unfamiliar. Thus Revelation 13 needs to be as much in the Christian consciousness as Romans 13, for in Revelation we see the full flowering of an arrogant imperial power demanding abject obedience. And—again it is important to note—in John's depiction in Revelation, it is not those who rise up in revolutionary violence like *Braveheart*'s William Wallace ("Freedom!") or the American patriots against the British ("Give me liberty or give me death!") who triumph. Instead, John maintains that it is those who bear witness to the Lamb through the sword of God's Word. It is those who are martyred who triumph over the evil empire. The persecuted ones, even in the midst of their own "axis of evil," are called not to make the world turn out right by employing the means and methods of empire, but the means and methods of the Lamb of God, trusting that God is

5. Cf. Cullmann, "Paul and the State," 65.

at work both in heaven and earth to bring about the triumph of God's kingdom.

A corollary to this claim is this: we cannot assume that whatever specific government or specific governmental policies exist are therefore specifically ordained by God.

In any case, as our manifesto has sought to make clear, we must not presume that governments alone may carry the mantle of political actor—a matter to which we now explicitly turn.

Christianity Is Not a Religion;
Christianity Is a Politic

SUMMARY

We will no longer say "Christianity is not political." When we say "Christianity is not political," we are only demonstrating that we are disciples of modern liberalism instead of disciples of Jesus. It is liberalism that has construed the world this way: (a) religion is a privately held set of beliefs pertaining to God or the afterlife or some such, and religion must be protected as an individual right so long as religion stays out of the realm of the public. (b) Christianity is a religion. (c) Therefore, Christianity is a private matter and is not, must not be, political.

But if religion is defined as liberalism would have it, then Christianity cannot possibly be a religion. The primary task of the Christian community is not to be a so-called religious gathering concerned with souls floating off into the afterlife, nor is it to be a sort of spiritualized yoga class helping individuals find existential peace with themselves. The primary task of the church is to embody and bear witness to the end of history, an all-compassing reality that has already broken into the world. The primary task of the church is to be an alternative politic. Jesus was clearly a political figure, calling his followers to a particular politic. His politic was a public claim and a public matter.

EXPOSITION

If we would be Christians in the world, as already argued, we must frame Christianity as an interpretation of human history that has history-changing and history-making power. This history-making and history-changing power is not concerned with the propagation of some religion by means of conventional powers of wealth, violence, or empire. In contrast, the political power of Christianity is not to be found in debt ("forgive us our debts, as we forgive our debtors") or retaliation ("pray for your enemies, do good to those who despitefully use you") or lording authority over others ("who being in very nature God did not count equality with God as a thing to be grasped").

We should be sensitive to the fact that non-Christians have good reason for wincing at any assertion that Christianity is political. Visions of Southern Christians showing up at the voting booth on their horses or with a twelve-gauge across their laps, with a Bible on the living room table, droning on piously about making America great again; such mockery is indeed wince-worthy. In such ways many Christians in politics have horribly misconstrued Christianity or misconstrued the political nature of Christianity. Christians themselves, as well meaning as they may or may not be, have often reduced the political nature of Christianity to some self-righteous religious moralism imposed through the power of the state: they have redacted the Christian story, pulling out bits of Christian values here and bits of "the Bible says" there.

Consequently, there are many good reasons to wince—even vociferously object—in response to someone claiming, "Christianity is inherently political." One good reason to object flows out of the false reduction of politics to the wheeling and dealing and machinations of partisan politics, especially at the federal level. Rightfully suspect of such, one may insist "Christianity ought not be political." They mean by this perhaps that we ought not get caught up in partisan politics, ought not get caught up in the struggle between Republicans and Democrats. If this is what one means, then it would be more truthful and helpful to say, "Christianity ought not be partisan."

To say "Christianity ought not be political" when one actually means "Christianity ought not be partisan" may lead innocent bystanders to believe a lie, namely, that the primary way to be political is to be either Republican or Democrat.

But to reduce our options for political to be either Republican or Democrat (or Tea Partier or socialist) represents opposite sides of the same American political coin. The question is how we may opt for an altogether different political currency.

Politics, classically understood, comprises the art and science of arranging the common goods of a community. Such a pursuit necessarily engages questions like these: What to do with enemies? What to do about marriage and families? How to deal with offenses and practices of reconciliation? How to handle practices of worship? How shall money, the pursuit of money, and the needs of the poor be addressed? How do we rightly conceive our work? What of liberty, appetites, and passions?

In providing a catalog of such political questions, what becomes so immediately obvious, but so incredibly ignored, is this: *the New Testament is clearly advocating an alternative politic, which is called "good news" for the world.*

(To say that one embraces an alternative politic by no means entails some wrongheaded withdrawal. Democrats and Republicans have alternative politics, one from the other, but the best of them still work alongside those in the other party, seeking bipartisan solutions to complex problems. There is no reason Christians, at their best, with their alternative politic cannot do the same. In fact, they must do the same.)

Again, it is easy to understand the fear of those terrified at the thought of Christianity being political. Visions arise of ISIS wielding their bloody swords and their mindless destruction of both human lives and cultural artifacts. And visions arise of Christianity run amuck, as already noted: Charlemagne's ruthless baptismal policy, in which the pagan Saxons could either come be baptized or be killed; the cross-bearing conquistadors butchering the indigenous population, hanging up body parts in the marketplace to feed their military attack dogs; the Nazi co-option of Christianity; Sermon-on-the-Mount-quoting President Truman who obliterated men, women, and children with his atom bombs.

But the problem with Charlemagne and Truman and the conquistadors was not that they mixed Christianity and politics. Instead, they failed to grasp, or live according to, the thoroughgoing nature of Jesus's politics. Their problem was reducing Christianity to something like what we mean by religion, something that informs our spirits, our private devotions to God, our personal spiritual commitments, but does not ultimately define our way in the world, does not ultimately define our political allegiance, does not ultimately determine the manner in which we comport ourselves among the peoples of the world, among our neighbors, among our enemies. Their problem was politicizing a highly redacted form of Christianity.

It is important to note the ways in which such moves have been important in getting access to means of power in American politics. A classic case of this was the election of John F. Kennedy, suspect because of his Catholicism. In a brilliant move—brilliant in terms of rhetorical caginess but devastating in terms of Christian theology—Kennedy addressed the Greater Houston Ministerial Association prior to the election in what proved to be a key moment in his election campaign. Therein he made his religion utterly private: "what kind of church I believe in," he insisted, "should be important only to me." "I believe in a president whose religious views are his own private affair."

Playing—appropriately—off the notion of the separation of church and state, Kennedy exhibits, however, the manner of separating the two that arises from classical political liberalism, instead of the sort of separation that arises out of an explicit commitment to the ways of Christ.

> I want a chief executive whose public acts are responsible to all groups and obligated to none; who can attend any ceremony, service or dinner his office may appropriately require of him;

and whose fulfillment of his presidential oath is not limited or conditioned by any religious oath, ritual or obligation.

Kennedy prioritizes what he believes is the best way to do nation-states, not what he takes to be grounded in the noncoercive ways of Christ.

Whatever issue may come before me as president—on birth control, divorce, censorship, gambling or any other subject—I will make my decision in accordance with these views, in accordance with what my conscience tells me to be the national interest, and without regard to outside religious pressures or dictates. And no power or threat of punishment could cause me to decide otherwise.

And he concludes, perhaps ironically, with noting that this sort of approach is grounded precisely in an oath to do so.

[If] I should win the election, then I shall devote every effort of mind and spirit to fulfilling the oath of the presidency—practically identical, I might add, to the oath I have taken for 14 years in the Congress. For without reservation, I can "solemnly swear that I will faithfully execute the office of president of the United States, and will to the best of my ability preserve, protect, and defend the Constitution, so help me God."[1]

This sort of misunderstanding of Christianity—as a privatized affair that has no authority truly to inform public life—sits well alongside what the theologians call "sacramentalism." Sacramentalism typically connotes an emphasis on the sacraments of the church—baptism, Eucharist, and the like—as very important pri-

---

1. All of these quotes are taken from "Transcript: JFK's Speech on His Religion," *National Public Radio*, December 5, 2007, https://www.npr.org/templates/story/story.php?storyId=16920600. Kennedy's original speech was given September 12, 1960.

marily because of their spiritual or religious or afterlife significance. They become akin to magic rites, totemic talismans: without baptism one will go to hell; with baptism one will not.

But the New Testament does not depict the church's sacraments as mere religious rituals, magical talismans intended to ensure the salvation of our souls in the afterlife. Instead, they are tangible means of the grace of God by which an alternative politic is gifted to us.

Baptism

Baptism is a voluntary induction into a new way of life in which our ultimate allegiance is to the lordship of Christ. His lordship teaches us how to tell the truth, love our enemies, keep our marriage vows, and share our wealth. *Baptism is the Christian's pledge of allegiance.* The voluntary nature of this commitment is itself a profound political alternative. Among the nations of the world, citizenship is a matter of the contingent particularities of one's birth; or may be dependent on current moods of those in power; or may be correlated with the degree to which the power brokers are predisposed to offer largesse to the immigrant or refugee.

But baptism—which is to say, induction into citizenship in the kingdom of God—is open to all, precisely because it is an induction into a community of hospitality.

Moreover, baptism is also an alternative political act in that it *explicitly transcends sociopolitical barriers.* The apostle Paul, for example, asserted that in Christ—which for him meant having been baptized "into Christ"—there was neither Jew nor Greek, no male and female, neither slave nor free. We could add other dividing walls of hostility in our own day: neither American nor Iraqi, neither rich nor poor, neither Caucasian nor African nor African American nor Hispanic, and the like. Such baptism constitutes what Paul calls a "new humanity," with a common and new ultimate allegiance.

(This claim should not be confused with a "melting pot" or "color-blind" approach which naively seeks to ignore difference and thereby privilege those in power. Instead, the move is precisely to relativize capricious power differentials and hostilities, overcome in the new allegiance to Christ.)

Baptism is consequently no mere religious ritual. It is a pledge of allegiance to trump all other pledges of allegiance. Thus when we are called to pledge allegiance to other political authorities, we must either reject such a call or do so only with a highly qualified pledge.

In any case, we must see the admonition of the president as a direct threat to Christian baptism: "At the bedrock of our politics will be a total allegiance to the United States of America, and through our loyalty to our country, we will rediscover our loyalty to each other."[2]

Preaching or Bearing Witness

Inherent in bearing witness are two profound political commitments.

First, the assumption that there is such a thing as truth. "You shall know the truth, and the truth shall set you free," said Jesus. All is not, must not, be reduced to spin. Our baptism inducts us into a community that rejects lying. The spinning of falsehoods is a grave offense against our neighbor. Thriving human communities necessitate vulnerability and risk, impossible without commitments to truth telling. The spinning of such falsehoods not only corrupts human community but is a grave offense against the God who is truth.

Bearing witness as a political practice then must not be reduced to a Sunday morning homily. Nor must it be reduced to venting on social media. To bear witness well is to tell the truth in such a way that new possibilities for human life, new possibilities for human relationship, new possibilities for social arrangements come into view. If our truth telling devolves merely into yet more hostile partisanship, then we have not yet sufficiently told or embodied the truth.

2. Donald Trump, "The Inaugural Address," *WhiteHouse.gov*, January 20, 2017, https://www.whitehouse.gov/briefings-statements/the-inaugural-address.

Second, the profound assumption inherent in bearing witness is the acceptance that my truth claims carry an inescapably subjective element. When I bear witness, I acknowledge that I am telling the truth as I understand it, telling the truth about my experience. This does not mean, cannot mean, that there is no such thing as truth, nor does it mean that we have no fair-minded access to it, at least in many cases. But because any bearing witness entails subjectivity, we must accept the contingency of our knowing; we are a mortal, finite, fallible species. We may be wrong. To bear witness rightly is, in other words, an exercise in humility.

Our bearing witness requires embracing a nonviolent form of living that says, among other things, "This is the way we see the world around us. We may be wrong; we are fallible. But this is what we see, and we see it by the light of a crucified and resurrected Messiah."

We should not take lightly the political gift that we may give the world by simply being able to model such humility and fallibility.

Eucharist

Much scholarship indicates the manner in which the Eucharist in the early church was not merely a religious ritual in the mode of sacramentalism. The Lord's Supper, instead, was a sacrament in which community and economic sharing and the tangible grace of God were all made manifest to the gathered, baptized community. The primary economic policy of the early church was not to advise the Roman Empire on imperialist tax policy but to practice a profound and generous sharing, modeled on the Old Testament practice of Jubilee, in which debts were forgiven and excess capital redistributed to those who most needed it.

It should go without saying but probably needs to be said, the fact that the community was voluntary, through its baptism, made viable such economic practices in a way that an involuntary community could not, still may not, likely imagine.

A great challenge for Christianity in the late-modern world, then, is to imagine the ways in which its sacraments—its means of God's grace to the world—can be enjoyed by a desperate and warring world. This can and should be done in the ways the church has traditionally administered the sacraments. And yet *we must set our imaginations free to put into play analogous practices in the surrounding world*. Just as the welcome table of Communion might serve, in our imagination, for the breaking down of the segregation of lunch counters in Nashville, so may Jubilee inform our imagination around laws of debt forgiveness for the poor, baptism inform our imagination around voluntary spaces of alternative conflict resolution, and Paul's counsel to the churches to let each one have his or her say, in a decent and orderly fashion, inform a commitment to a free press.

But above all, we must not misconstrue the sacraments as so-called religious practices that can be separated from so-called political practices; this misconstrues not only the sacraments but Christianity.

One classic case of the bastardization of the sacraments is the infamous tale of the Christmas truce in World War I. The Germans were arrayed on one side, the French and British on the other; a no-man's-land stretched between the trenches that troops had dug into the French countryside, ditches filled with "mud and blood and vermin," an ant hill–like network in which the troops could stay below ground to avoid bullets shot from the other side.

On Christmas Eve, a truce had been called to honor the birth of Jesus. The kaiser had sent Christmas trees to the German troops; the British and French had sent gifts and care packages to their own. In an unfathomable development, someone trotted a Christmas tree out into the no-man's-land. Before long, a soccer game was engaged between mortal enemies, played on this bit of land between the trenches. Gifts and chocolates were shared, a squeeze box and fiddle contributed melodies, and some Germans began singing "Stille Nacht," and the English joined in with their own "Silent Night."

On Christmas Day, Eucharist was shared by these mortal enemies. They shared a common baptism and thus shared a com-

Christmas Truce, artist's impression from *The Illustrated London News,* January 9, 1915. *A. C. Michael. Wikimedia Commons*

mon meal, remembering the death of their Christ and the graces received thereby.

The next day they resumed their killing. Some fifteen million were killed in World War I, most of them at least nominally Christian, fighting on behalf of nominally Christian nations.

This historical account—and our assessment of this shocking historical incident—tells us a great deal about the status of Christianity in the Western world. There are sentimentalists who can celebrate the fact that in the midst of a tragic world some sort of universal or religious truth could temporarily suspend the warring madness.

But such sentimentality will not suffice. Let us see the incident as a parable for the manner in which modernity and the gods of the nation-states have co-opted Christian practice. Such bastardized moments of so-called religion communicate something like this: you may take thirty-six hours for a truce, do your religious thing, and then we'll get back to the real business of human history.

Thereby the nation-state, propped up by its modernist privatization of religion, guts Christianity of the substance of its faith—that is, a community of peoples reconciled unto God and thereby unto one another through the gracious power and forgiveness of God. Thereby, the rites of the Christian faith are treated like playthings while the rites of the respective militaries are treated like real things.

It is important to note, yet again, that this is not some leftist critique of America, for on the killing fields of World War I were all sorts of nominally Christian nations—English, French, German, American—and the rites of those nation-states trumped the rites of the church. We would-be Christians must not only learn to embody our own rituals as if they are the real thing; we must learn not to play at the rituals and rites of the nation-state.

Indeed, one might conjecture that while the World War I truce was an exhibition of the marginalization of the Eucharist and baptism, or, as noted, a sentimentalization of the meaning of Christmas, it was nonetheless at least a token of such. Moreover, in those days on those battlefields, we caught glimpses, too, of the natural human aversion to killing, in which many soldiers would shoot over the heads of their opponents, deliberately choosing not to kill the enemy. And yet it has been through ritual, practice, and training that this very aversion to killing has been overcome. The US military has studied and implemented forms of practice to overcome this natural aversion, so that troops may learn to kill in a desensitized fashion, increasing the rate at which combat infantry were willing to shoot to kill, from 15 to 25 percent in World War II to 90 percent in the Vietnam War.[3]

The sacraments, by contrast, are intended to form us into a particular kind of people who share gracious, risky hospitality, abundant generosity, and long-suffering patience. The sacraments are to be our own alternative forms of practice, at which we work for the whole of our lives.

---

3. See Dave Grossman, *On Killing: The Psychological Cost of Learning to Kill in War and Society* (Boston: Little, Brown, 1995).

Liberal Political Puissance
Is Not the Goal

SUMMARY

The primary task of Christian community is not to dominate
the political communities that do not accept basic Christian
claims. Our task is not to dominate the debates between liberal
liberals and the conservative liberals, to forcibly bring to bear
some redacted form of Christian values on a system that knows
not Christ. To pursue such dominance would, in fact, be a rejection of basic Christian faith and practice. We live in an out-
of-control fashion precisely because we serve a Messiah who
had no messianic complex but who first and foremost obeyed
the will of God, even if it meant losing, even if it meant getting
himself killed.

EXPOSITION

The primary task of the community of Christians is not to run the
unbelieving world, is not to dominate the political communities
that do not accept basic Christian claims. Two reasons for this are
straightforward and will provide the outline of this chapter. First,
ultimate and radical liberty provides the ground of Christianity.
Second, ultimate and radical liberty must also characterize any and
all means of the spread of Christianity.

These claims are of great importance. They allow us clearly to see that many of the arguments about Christian values turn out to be a bastardized form of Christianity precisely because of the use of and reliance on coercive power. But any morality, practice, or conviction imposed through violence cannot be, by definition, a Christian morality, practice, or conviction. Christianity is a call to divest itself of such forms of power.

An Ultimate and Radical Liberty Provides the Ground of Christian Faith and Practice

Even prior to the coming of the Christ, Israel knew that our God is a God of steadfast love whose love endures forever. The covenant relationship with Israel was grounded in a love that allowed Israel to "go whoring after other lovers." Beyond Israel, all peoples have been given the liberty to reject the call of God. All people have been given the liberty to reject all that is right and good and beautiful.

This is not to say—and this is a terribly important caveat—that there are no consequences for such rejection. One may ignore, say, the nature of social relations or the tendencies of particular political commitments or the field of gravity. But in each of these cases there are consequences for one's ignorant choices.

But the nature of God's covenant relationship with Israel—in spite of the radical liberty granted Israel to reject the steadfast love of God—nonetheless entailed a place of deep coercion. Israel participated in, and the God of Israel participated in, practices of violence and coercion. This appears to be true, at a minimum, because Israel was founded as a geographically bounded nation. Given that Israel's God was committed to Israel's flourishing in the world as a light to the nations, and given that human history was bloody and violent, and given that survival as a geographically bounded nation entailed practices of war, this God of Israel got his hands dirty, we might say. Precisely because this God was not unconcerned with the injustices of the mighty and the violence of the wicked, this God refused to allow the wicked and the unjust to overthrow God's people. Thus, the geographically bounded Israel coincided with the legitimation of, even call to, war.[1]

But even within this qualified acceptance of war, the prophets depicted a coming day of a new peaceableness in which swords would be beaten into plowshares and swords into pruning hooks and the nations would learn war no more.

Thus, with the coming of Messiah a new model of kingship was chosen. Not one in which history no longer mattered in favor of some spiritual kingship. This Messiah was a new David, a true king, indeed even King of kings. He compared to emperors, who called themselves sons of the gods, for he was heralded the Son of God. And yet, as the prophet foretold, kings "shut their mouths" because of him. He came among us as one who does not break a bruised reed or extinguish a barely flickering wick. He does not bear the rod of iron of the kings of old but suffers the blows that were all ours to bear. The distinctive of his alternative kingship is not that it is spiritual—many of the kings and presidents and prime ministers have their own spirituality, after all. Instead, his alternative kingship is located precisely in the manner of his bearing of authority: the gentiles, he said, lord authority. But among you, it shall not be so. You shall be servants of all, not lords of all.

This Jesus was not crucified because he was spiritual. He was crucified because he incarnated a new way of being king and a new way of being human, a new way that terrifies even the most spiritual of kings and presidents and prime ministers to this day.

In addition to this new model of kingship, this new people would *not* be geographically bounded. This people is drawn from every tribe, every land, every nation. This is one of the great political facts of Christianity often overlooked and often ignored with regard to the rush to war. For when one nation makes war against another, it is often, very often, Christians in one nation killing Christians in another.

1. See proposition 6, note 5, regarding Peter Craigie's work, whose argument I am relying on here.

This great political fact is ignored in other aspects, say in our walls and boundary building. Given that we live "between the times," it may be legitimate for a nation-state to have a protected border, even though any and all borders clearly stand in opposition to the end of history. And given that we Christians are the people who bear witness, in our common life together, to the end of history, we Christians cannot first and foremost be concerned with a border but must be more concerned with our neighbor on either side of that border, must be more concerned with our brother and sister with whom we share baptism on either side of that border. Walls and borders and national self-interest must always be granted only provisional, contingent importance, and not an ultimate one.

One important objection: Jesus and the early church told tales of coming judgment. And these depictions of judgment are inherently violent. Are such visions not coercive, at least psychologically? Might one even say that the pictures of coming destruction are religiously abusive?

Perhaps. It may be, as some scholars have claimed, that some of the writers of Scripture failed, themselves, to sufficiently comprehend the radical nature of the revelation of God in Christ and continued to employ old apocalyptic visions of punishment that stand at odds with the newness revealed in Christ.

While this is an objection worthy of note, another significant possibility runs in a different direction. To posit the theological construct of judgment is to say something we know to be true, that there are consequences for our injustice, our violence, our greed. On the one hand these consequences may be what we might call natural. The horrors that come upon us may be the natural outgrowth of our own rebellion and failings and self-centered and systemically propagated longings after wealth and power and pleasure.

The liberal liberal hankering after a sexuality with no boundaries or a conservative liberal hankering after a market with no boundaries both show themselves as naive as the little boy who insists gravity does not pertain to him. His insistence may be altogether sincere as he jumps from his tree house with the conviction that he may fly by flapping his arms. But there will be consequences, and wishful thinking cannot will them away.

This is one crucial way to configure the necessity of judgment.

On the other hand, to uphold the theological importance of judgment may be a fulfillment of the human longing that the Creator of all things would in fact judge. Only the naive or philosophically adolescent desires no judgment. Once we have seen or suffered or witnessed oppression, we most undoubtedly want judgment. This longing for judgment need not be a rapacious longing for vengeance or retaliation. But it is surely deep within us to long that the Creator of all things would definitively pronounce, would establish with all authority and finality,

> Joy, not *bitterness*.
> Love, not *hostility*.
> Life, not *death*.
> *This*, not *that*.

Some sort of depiction of judgment as this must arise out of the claim of a crucified and resurrected Lord.

While it should be clear already, it may be helpful to note again that this call to nonviolence is most certainly *not* a call to passivity or codependence or any form of cowardly shrinking away from injustice or oppression. We are not called to let others run over us, and we must not equate "turning the other cheek" with any such passivity. Jesus enkindled within his followers a fertile imagination to look for a third way between violence and passivity, between retaliation and running away.

An Ultimate and Radical Liberty Must Also Characterize Any and All Means of the Spread of Christianity

An apple tree does not yield lemons, and one gets to an oak only by the acorn. In the same way, the fruit of authentic Christianity comes only by means of the divestment of coercion and violence.

The name commonly given to the temptation to impose Christianity on the world is Constantinianism. Constantine was the Roman emperor who made Christianity a legal religion, banning persecution of Christians. (This latter fact is, of course, something to celebrate.) But Constantine's nominal acceptance of Christianity (he appears to have remained a rather cold-blooded emperor who finally accepted baptism on his deathbed) meant first that the means of empire began to be commingled with the church.

By the end of the fourth century, Christianity was made, under Emperor Theodosius, the only legal religion in the empire. This entailed a radical social change. Within one century Christianity went from being officially persecuted under Emperors Decius and Diocletian at the end of the third century to being the only legal religion, and one thus could be persecuted for practicing some other religion, by the end of the fourth century. Moreover, up until the end of the third century, all extant writings from the church fathers exhibit the consistent and unanimous rejection of Christians killing in warfare, but by a century later one had to be a baptized Christian in order to be a member of the Roman military. By the time of Christmas Day 800 CE, with the coronation of Charlemagne came the outrageous employment of imperial violence in service to baptism. You can either be baptized, said Charlemagne, or we will kill you.

Of course, this sort of bastardized form of medieval European Christianity would exhibit its own particular horrors when it would come to the Americas. Bartolomé de las Casas, a Dominican priest who witnessed firsthand some of the work of the conquistadors, concedes it is not possible sufficiently to describe the atrocities, so great was the terror. He documented how the Spanish conquistadors would tear babies from their mothers' breasts and smash their brains on the rocks. When those sixteenth-century Christians arrived in the Americas, they also brought with them their dogs, unleashed to hunt the indigenous as if they were wild pigs. They would cast women and children into pits full of stakes, impaled until the pit was full. They would gather together hundreds of natives and then systematically massacre them, sparing none, and meanwhile tie up the leading citizens, dangling them from gibbets, their feet just above the ground, and roast them alive. They set up butcher shops, hacking up the men and women, selling their parts for food for dogs.

The conquests entailed cultural domination as well. The *Requerimiento* aptly symbolizes such cultural violence. Arriving to conquer some new people, the conquistadors would read aloud the *Requerimiento*. The proclamation would be read in Spanish (which, obviously, the indigenous population did not understand) and required them to accept the rule of Spanish Christian kings, because the pope had, after all, granted such dominion and sovereignty to the Spanish monarchy. They could accept such terms, so the proclamation announced, or face war, slavery, or death. Furthermore, they would insist that any deaths that followed were the fault of the natives for not accepting Spanish Christian rule.

Meanwhile, back in the great halls of academia in Europe, the churchmen were debating whether the natives were in fact people, were in fact human, or not.[2]

It is too simple and too naive to say, Oh, we know better than those medieval barbarians; we have separation of church and state.

---

2. It is worth noting that numerous twentieth-century academics would decry the "Black Legend" arising out of the sixteenth century that the opponents of Spain would blacken the reputation of Spain and never take account of any of the cultural goods having arisen from Spaniards. Such a move, such academics note, serves a sociopolitical function: decrying the crimes of one's enemies, noting only their atrocities, makes warring against them more feasible, even desirable. This is an important observation that serves as an illustration of the fact that the demonization of a tradition, party, or ideology that one hates is easy enough and illustrates further why some sort of practice of identifying the principalities and powers, apart from mere reduction to some mortal or national or sectarian enemy ("our enemies are not flesh and blood," says Ephesians when speaking of the powers), is fundamentally important if we Christians are not to fall prey to the sorts of horrors here decried. Instead, note this: Bartolomé de las Casas was himself both a male European, Spanish, and Christian. Based on his work within the Spanish Christian tradition, a hold-no-punches indictment of the horrors of his fellow men, did Spanish Christians begin to reassess their horrors, for which many had no moral convictions to lead them to question their actions.

Theodore de Bry, depiction of Spanish atrocities in the New World, 16th century. *Wikimedia Commons*

The matter is more subtle and dangerous than that for the Christian. The issue is not simply whether to post the Ten Commandments in the Supreme Court House of Alabama or to enforce a policy of school prayer or some such explicit so-called religious practice or totem. It is the Constantinian logic that is of greater danger: if our goal is legitimate, then state-sanctioned coercive violence is a legitimate means toward that end. It is often the secularists who find great allies among the Constantinians on this score. Democracy and capitalism must prevail; thus by hook or by crook we shall prevail, and we will not go down without a fight to coercively enforce our will upon the world: whether tromping from sea to shining sea based on some delusion of Manifest Destiny; whether by subversion of the legitimately elected president of Chile, leading to the ruthless Pinochet dictatorship; whether by propagation of the promise of a world conflagration if we are threatened with the very weapons that we alone have employed, as in the rise of the US policy of MAD—"mutually assured destruction" by means of nuclear weapons; or whether by a state of perpetual war, as that in which we now find ourselves, our drones as fiery manifestation from the sky of judge, jury, and executioner. The issue is whether we Christians explicitly set aside the teachings of Jesus in order to effect some desirable social end; whether we will take seriously as a sociopolitical stance Jesus's insistence that it is the gentiles who lord authority over others, but that it is not to be so among us; or Jesus's teaching that we should love our enemies, pray for those who abuse us, and forgive seventy times seven; or Jesus's proclamation that the kingdom of heaven comes by mercy and peacemaking and truth telling and a willingness to suffer in the pursuit of the new order of God in the world.

Our prophetic voice must be raised in protest against those who carry the name of Christ yet ignore the way of Christ.

Even more, our kerygmatic voice of proclaiming, winsomely, the constructive alternative of the gospel must be raised in the public square. For

> Your responsibility is a "to—":
> you can never save yourself by a "not to."[3]

And so it is not sufficient for us to contend that our primary task is *not* this or that. We Christians with our moralisms and petty finger-wagging have done enough damage to our witness in the world and must move to a more constructive task: to show the world what the beautiful and spectacular world was in fact made to be.

---

3. Dag Hammarskjöld, *Markings*, trans. Leif Sjöberg and W. H. Auden (New York: Alfred A. Knopf, 1964), 98.

Exemplary Political Witness Is the Goal

SUMMARY

While our task is *not* liberal political puissance, is not to make things turn out right, is not to "make America great again," and is not to run the world, it is nonetheless a grand and majestic calling to the world: to bear witness to the world, even to the powers of the world, what the world was intended to be, and what it shall be when the consummation of the end of history comes.

But how to navigate the messy relations between church and world? Three historical models are considered here, providing clues for constructive work as well as signs of potential dangers.

EXPOSITION

As said repeatedly by now, we are seeking to fashion a politic neither right nor left nor religious. In the New Testament, the church is not some religious club. Instead, we repeatedly see instances in which the church embodies an alternative politic. In fact, claims the letter to the Ephesians, it is "through the church the wisdom of God in its rich variety might now be made known to the rulers and authorities" (Eph. 3:10). If indeed it is the calling of the people of God to exhibit the wisdom of God to the principalities and powers, the next obvious question of *how* turns out to be a hotly debated one in the Christian tradition. What is the social shape, the rightful ordering of our common life, such that God's wisdom may be exhibited to the world, may be exhibited to the powers?

The Christian tradition has exhibited a great plurality in this regard. Three examples are given here, each of which will simultaneously provide exemplars and counterexemplars.

A Stereotypical Medieval Catholic Stance

In medieval Christendom, the teachings of Jesus, especially the so-called hard teachings of Jesus, are reserved for a special elite called "religious." The religious have a special vocation, have taken vows to keep the challenging teachings of Jesus. Meanwhile, the mass of nominal Christians in the world are not expected to keep such demanding teachings. As one example, priests were expected not to participate in warfare, while laymen were expected to do so if the war was thought justifiable according to the tradition of the so-called just war tradition. Then, such laymen were expected— because the church took seriously that war was always an evil and never to be glibly celebrated—to undergo practices of penance when returning home even from a justifiable war, given that they had shed blood.

The rise of monasticism can be interpreted, and has been by some, as a moment of renewal in the life of the Christian tradition. The mass of nominal Christianity had grown so unchristian that some believed it necessary to develop their own intentional communities to facilitate a common life in Christ. The monastic move can be deeply appreciated in this regard. And it could be a viable option in numerous historical contexts, just as some are calling for a reappropriation of this sort of witness today in the diverse and varied movement of new monasticism.

This overall approach, however, taken on the whole, lends itself to a grave fragmentation of Christian witness. In numerous instances it leads simply to setting aside the way of Christ. The Norman Conquest of England in 1066 by William the Conqueror provides a classic example. William goes to war carrying the pope's ring as a sign of the pope's blessing and assurance that the war is justified. William is ruthless and bloody, and his infamous "Harrying of the North" lays waste shires, burns buildings, murders villagers, and slaughters livestock. He conquers with little mercy. And he is memorialized in the choir screen in magnificent York Minster, a tribute to kings, too often carrying about a nominal Christian faith with their bloody swords. Or in London the quaint chapel in the White Tower in the midst of the celebrated Tower of London—that foreboding and impressive architectural monument to ruthless power and decapitation and imperial power suffused with the Christian religion—serves as a living reminder of this sociopolitical interpretation of Christianity.

While this approach presents grave shortcomings—so much so that in many instances we may find it difficult to call it Christian—there remain significant gifts that arose from the social strategies of Christendom.

For one, Christendom models have taken seriously fostering relative political goods. While the hospital in the West may be traced back at least to the Roman military, it was Christendom that began to make hospitals available to civilians; they were often attached to monasteries. Similarly, systems of education, particularly the universities, would not be what they are today apart from the preservation of such goods in Christendom. And while much early scientific research is indebted to Muslim scholars, the promulgation of much scientific inquiry is also indebted to the complex and extensive forms of human goods made possible by Christendom. *The Christendom model insists, we might say, that relative political goods are of great importance.* Even if particular goods may not exhibit the fullness of Christian faith and practice and confession, they remain true goods of life and community, and we do well to engender and foster them.

There are many gifts given by God's grace that remain good whether one professes the lordship of Christ or not, and thus we must not fail to participate in the cultivation of such goods in whatever ways afforded us.

A second exemplary gift of Christendom is *its ability to check the power of rulers.* In spite of the problems with the attempt to wed coercive power to the church—or if not wed it, to find some sort of too-easy alliance between the two—one of the great strengths of this approach was the manner in which the church could, when it chose to exercise such courage, chastise and discipline the wayward ruler. While famed cases like Thomas Becket, with his own harrying of the powers that be through means of excommunication, are complicated and complex, there is nonetheless therein a sort of integrity and courage that should be remembered: that we dare not let rulers—especially those who claim to be Christian— off the hook easily. Henry II's exasperation with Becket, exemplified in the legendary words he uttered to his aides—"who will rid me of this turbulent priest?"—finally led to Becket's demise, a nasty murder by four knights with Becket's blood and brains smeared on the stones of the floor of Canterbury Cathedral.

This was, of course, the reason that Protestants in America distrusted John F. Kennedy as a Catholic. They feared he would be under obligation to the pope or other church hierarchy. A good patriotic Protestant will have none of that. And, following the narrative given in proposition 11, Kennedy turned out to be more Protestant than Catholic on this score.

Luther and the Protestant Reformation

With the Protestant Reformation, another general posture is discernible. For Martin Luther the key dividing line does not run between two classes of people in the church, between the religious and the lay. The key dividing line, we might say, runs through every individual. Thus, Luther draws a sharp distinction between the secular and the spiritual, between the inner self and what one does in the world.

The Sermon on the Mount, for Luther, pertains to the realm of the inner man and personal relationships. But it does not apply to the realm of the secular. For Luther the secular and one's vocational roles in the secular have their own ethical logic. If one is called to be a lord or a lady, then, in effect, says Luther, read the job manual. But don't read the Sermon on the Mount.[1] If one is called to be an executioner, the lord will tell you what to do, and you should do it and not think that you are violating Christian duty, because the Sermon on the Mount does not pertain to what one does in the secular realm but only within oneself and in one's personal relationships. So: if you must decapitate, do so, and do so while loving in one's heart (but not with one's sword) the one who is being decapitated. Luther thereby fragments Christianity in his own way. The Christian witness lacks integrity within every soul.

This privatization of Christian faith has done immense harm. And yet there are other potential failings with this approach, perhaps even more harmful.

First, Luther may be seen as sowing the seeds of a deep sociopolitical conservatism that may pit the governing authorities against those who plead for justice against oppression. He himself railed against the peasants who cried out for justice against the rich and the mighty. He called on Christians to take up their swords to "stab, smite, and slay" the peasants who had themselves taken up the cause of armed rebellion. More frightening, one might make the case that Luther's anti-Semitism, when sown amidst the seeds of his implicit sociopolitical conservatism, plowed the ground for the social conservatism that gave Lutheran Germany the plague of Nazism, though Luther undoubtedly would have decried that madness, just as he had insisted that a Christian soldier ought never obey an unjust order by a superior. He worthily considered and set forward criteria for the proper occasions for civil disobedience.

Second, Luther and the Protestant Reformation fragmented Christianity in yet another deeply disturbing way: the rise of the nation-state. Coupled with the rise of modernity, the Reformation

---

1. This sort of distinction runs throughout Luther's *Commentary on the Sermon on the Mount*, trans. Charles Augustus Hay (Philadelphia: Lutheran Publication Society, 1892), https://archive.org/details/commentaryonsermooluth.

helped fragment Christianity by means of the rise of the nation-state in that each Christian becomes susceptible to pledging allegiance to his or her own local authorities. Given that the nation-state takes, typically, a role of self-interest with regard to its own survival and success, this allegiance pits a Christian in one land against a Christian in another. (The very sociopolitical meaning of baptism is thus subverted.)

With Luther privatizing fundamental Christian witness to the realm of the spiritual and the personal, the nation-state takes on the role of historical Messiah, takes on the role of the primary bearer of the meaning of history. Seeds of the bastardization of Christian hope are thereby sown. Christians become willing to slaughter, in vast numbers, other Christians in service to their local, sectarian allegiances. Even where I sit while writing these words, bullets flew and bayonets killed not many decades ago, the Union Christian struck down his fellow baptized Confederate, and the Confederate brother made a widow of his Union sister in Christ.

The relatively primitive nature of that sort of killing of Christians by Christians in service to their sectarian allegiances was, nonetheless, something that gave way to a new thing in the history of warfare in the West: the rise of total war, in which civilian populations become the legitimate target of military violence. It was a development that both medieval Christendom and the Protestant Reformation would have rightly decried. The just war tradition, after all, ruled out such grotesque forms of violence. But the totalization of war and privatization of Christian faith would only grow more perverse with the rise of industrialization, by which nominally Christian nations aligned themselves one against the other. The blood-spattered and vermin-infested trenches of World War I would in time yield to the horrors of World War II, in which the sociopolitical conservatism and anti-Semitism of Luther, sown into the soil of the nation-state and love of fatherland (again, well beyond anything he would have ever imagined or in any way desired) would yield the fruit of Nazism. Christians on all sides pledged their sociopolitical allegiance to their own nation-state while pledging a privatized spirituality in their hearts, and out of such a divided household strove with all possible industrialized efficiency to kill the Christian on the other side of the arbitrary line drawn by the powers that be.

(The hypothetical question, What about Hitler? is often raised as a sort of rhetorical dismissal of taking seriously nonviolent Christian witness. But other hypothetical questions are certainly just as apropos: What if German Christians had refused to fall prey to the dangers of nationalism? What if German Christians had refused to propagate anti-Semitism? What if German Christians had refused to take up the sword for the fatherland because their baptism was more important than their national identity?)[2]

Yet to be fair to Luther, his insistence on such a posture is grounded in a desire to preserve the relative goods of social order. The "orders of creation," he insists, are gifts to preserve life and society. There are numerous points to be lauded in the integrity by which he seeks to hold this desire along with Christian allegiance. As one poignant example, Luther insists that social order is more important than one's own personal existence. Consequently, he says, personal self-defense is no reason to set aside the Sermon on the Mount. It shows too great an attachment to one's own life.

And there is another tradition extending from Lutheranism that can provide us immense help: the notion of realism, which insists that we take realistically the sinful nature of human history. The question, however, is whether we may employ such realism without falling prey to Luther's other failings.

The Radical Reformation and the Anabaptists

A third form of Christian life is seen in the so-called Anabaptist model. The Anabaptists were called such because they, so far as their Catholic and Lutheran antagonists were concerned, were

2. For an extensive look at these sorts of questions, see the fine book by Robert Brimlow, *What about Hitler? Wrestling with Jesus's Call to Nonviolence in an Evil World* (Grand Rapids: Brazos Press, 2006).

"baptizing again." Infant baptism had become the sociopolitical-religious means of induction into Christendom, into the practice of a nominal Christianity. The Anabaptists understood clearly, on the other hand, that adult believer baptism is a significant sociopolitical act: it allows adults a voluntary choice to reject or accept Christian faith and practice.

Adult believer baptism, in that context, was accounted a pushback against the assumptions of Christendom. It granted a believer a substantive voluntary will in taking up Christian faith and taking up the way of the nonviolent Jesus. This was a threat to both Lutheran and Catholic models of the day, which presumed the legitimacy of Christendom. To allow individuals to choose against the nominal Christianity of Christendom was a threat to the very social fabric. Thus Luther angrily insisted that these radicals should set their aim to denounce the pope, not infant baptism. The radicals, however, would not accept the self-contradictory rejection of the authority of Christ. One of the leaders, Peter Chelčický, satirized those who would balk "at eating pork on Friday but who saw nothing wrong with human slaughter any day of the week."[3]

The radicals, as they have come to be known in histories of the Reformation, were enough of a threat that they were hunted down, persecuted, tried, and executed in demeaning ways: tongues cut out, flesh torn with red-hot tongs, burned alive, decapitated, or tied with ropes, stones affixed to the ends of the rope, and thrown into the river. The irony and tragedy are thick in that these Christians were executed and demeaned by other Christians in a deep struggle regarding the rightful political shape of Christian witness.

(And to put more of a point on it: it is too easy for Christians to act as if it is the secularists or the so-called liberals who have somehow duped Christians into falling prey to forsaking the way of Christ. It is very often Christians themselves, often the official

---

3. Peter Chelčický, quoted in Donald Durnbaugh, *The Believers' Church: The History and Character of Radical Protestantism* (Scottdale, PA: Herald Press, 1985), 255–56.

Jan Luyken (1649–1672), *Execution by Fire of Anneken Hendriks in* *Amsterdam, 1571,* **17th century.** *Wikimedia Commons*

apparatus of church hierarchy, who are duping the church into its own unfaithfulness.)

These Anabaptists were, of course, heralds of the way forward. Their insistence that the church had to yield its old Constantinian and Christendom presumptions would in time become conventional wisdom. They, of course, did not insist this for the same reasons that the spokespersons of modern liberalism articulated. The latter wanted to marginalize the church in service to other goals: individual autonomy or the triumph of the secular state. Anabaptists, on the other hand, wanted Christians to prioritize the way of Christ in all realms of life.

These radicals insisted on a voluntary community of believers who would be an outpost of the present-and-coming kingdom of God. They would, in their life together, seek to exhibit the reconciling and suffering love of God to the world. Their task, to use the language of the twentieth-century Georgian Clarence Jordan, was to be a demonstration plot exhibiting what it might look like to let the seeds of God's goodness be grown in our midst. The persuasive power of the gospel had to be located, for these radicals, in its winsomeness, not in its terror.

This strand of Christian witness has insisted that their task is not to run the world, is not to make the world safe for democracy or free-market capitalism; their task was first and foremost to embody the way of God in the world revealed in Jesus of Nazareth. Thus, they insisted on certain particulars that were a great threat to the Christendom of their day. They would tell the truth and not play games with oaths. They would make allegiance only to the lordship of Christ and no prince or ruler of this world. They would allow, as noted, the free acceptance or rejection of the good news of God's coming into the world through adult, believer baptism. They would not take up the sword against the enemies of Christendom or their own personal enemies but seek to love them.

Some discount the radical tradition as a form of wrongheaded withdrawal. Before considering this claim at some length in the next chapter, we may note that the body of Christ is gifted with a variety of giftings. Thus the Amish withdrawal to rural agrarian life or the monastic withdrawal to pray in the hills of Kentucky both may make significant contributions to the Christian witness in American culture. But we need not see this sort of withdrawal as *the* faithful form of Christian witness or even as the *primary* form of the radical witness. Surely particular communities of Christians might, however difficult it may be, find ways to bear witness to the grace of the gospel in a great variety of social contexts.

There are in fact plenty of examples from within the radical tradition in which a different posture prevailed. These saw that their greatest contribution to so-called civil society could be made neither in privatizing their faith nor in spiritualizing away the import of the Sermon on the Mount or setting aside the way of Christ—but that their greatest contributions could be made precisely in holding onto all these things in public. In fact, the case has been made that this tradition played a key role in the development of modern democracies. Durnbaugh observes, "One point that must be made is that the effect of the life and witnesses of the Believers' Churches helped create modern western democracy. It can even be said that these groups have made their most effective contributions to politics by their faithful, even stubborn, adherence to their religious views."[4]

But one of the key differences with the Lutheran and Constantinian traditions lies here: that even when, for example, the Quakers were tasked with local governance, they refused to set aside the teachings of Christ, thereby refusing to participate in the war making that was expected of them.[5]

This must be one characteristic of an alternative politic neither right nor left nor religious: that the authority of Christ is trumped by no other. It will require, for example, an explicit rejection of Luther's ethic of vocation as well as a rejection of a Constantinian watering down of the way of Christ. From this single simple but far-reaching conviction—that the authority of Christ is trumped by no other—there is a great diversity and plurality of faithful witness.

This vision might be best encapsulated by the vision of the prophet Jeremiah to the Jews in Babylonian exile: "seek the peace of the city wherein you dwell," he said (Jer. 29:7). There is the fact of exile, the fact of a distinct divergence of commitments and values and goals and peoplehood between the Jews and the Babylonians. And yet this fact does not preclude fertile, even joyous, participation in "the city." We are called to seek the peace of the city, and we do so precisely through our own cultural contributions to the communities in which we live.

Some may understandably object. All this talk of the church as exemplary, as providing an alternative sociopolitical witness to

---

4. Durnbaugh, *Believers' Church*, 260–61.

5. Durnbaugh is the classic text recounting the history of the varied radical or believers church traditions. He deals with the Quakers on church and state questions in chapter 10.

the waiting world, is nothing but wishful thinking, so great is the hypocrisy and failings of the church. (And, in fact, my storytelling here has indicated some of these grave failings.)

This is a weighty objection. The particular failings of the church in the twentieth and early twenty-first centuries pose a great indictment on Christianity in the Western world. The militarism, racism, sexism, homophobia, and conspicuous consumption—not to mention the horrific scandals of abuse or other grotesque forms of marginalization—have too often been propagated if not celebrated by a large part of the Christian church. All these failings remain not merely as a stain but as a deep wound on the church.

Of course, we must not confuse *church* with any given institutional configuration. But this observation must not become an easy out, an easy way to avoid a serious critique.

The following are three brief considerations with regard to the failings of the church.

1. A primary place to focus some of our concern is with the church itself, not for the sake of the church but for the sake of the world. If the church takes seriously the formation of its own—including, obviously, those in various leadership roles in the church—then we may do a great deal of good for the world by inhibiting some of the damage we have done to the world. "A Modest Proposal for Peace," lines the head of an old peacemakers' poster, "That the Christians of the World Will Not Kill Each Other." Not merely not kill one another but also not abuse, demean, or objectify one another, and beyond the "do no harm" starting point we will learn to do good to one another.

2. We must accept that the charges of hypocrisy are true. The charge of hypocrisy, in some measure, will *always* be true because we live between the times. Our attempts at proleptic living will always fall short of that which we proclaim to believe. But to accept the charge of hypocrisy as true can then lead in one of two directions: (1) a sort of glib acceptance that "we are all bastards but God loves us anyway," or (2) a sort of chastened and joyous path toward truth telling about ourselves: "yes, we are indeed all

bastards, but God loves us anyway and calls us to keep growing, yearning, changing." This latter course opens up the necessity of learning to tell the truth about ourselves and learning to tell the truth about our failings. In this process of truth telling we may become an example to a world that desperately needs spaces and practices of such authenticity, for only such authenticity can lead to genuine freedom.

3. There is no guaranteed method to do church without the risk of grave failure. But this does not mean we have been left without gifts and promises. For example, the promise that God would sustain the people of God and that the gates of hell would not prevail against it. The promise that Christ would never leave us or forsake us. The promise of the Holy Spirit, ever convicting, enlivening, and making all things new. And the gifts of Eucharist and baptism and proclamation and all the varied charisms of the body.

Out of such promises and gifts we need not fall prey, then, to despair, even though the failings of the church are so grave. Just as we must not, living between the times, fall prey to ideological political partisanship, so must we not fall prey to idealizing the church. But such a realism leaves us then with a more solid grounding—that this is not an easy calling, risk free, guaranteed to be faithful. But we have been promised that we would not be left alone, not be left friendless, and not be left without daily graces.

Christianity Is Not Countercultural

SUMMARY

The conventional wisdom among some Christian subcultures that Christianity is countercultural exhibits an ignorance regarding terms. More, it fails to say anything clarifying or constructive. Withdrawal from culture, further, is not simply a bad strategy; it is a logical fallacy. Similarly, charges of sectarianism often confuse more than they clarify and require careful analysis. Instead of a stance that is countercultural, a practice of percipient cultural discernment proves more constructive and clarifying.

EXPOSITION

To summarize to this point: Christianity claims that history has a direction, a meaning, an endgame in which all things will be set to rights. More, Christianity claims that the end of history has already begun, has been inaugurated in the birth, ministry, death, burial, resurrection, and ascension of the Christ. As the blind will receive their sight, the nations will learn war no more, and the dead will be raised, so down payments of the resurrecting power of God have broken into the midst of human history even now. Those who call on the name of Christ are to be the ongoing incarnation, the body of Christ, embodying this alternative politic in the world. They are to live a proleptic politic.

To envision the nation-state—any nation-state—as the primary bearer of the salvific work of God in the world is to bastardize the Christian hope. But American Christians—because they have too often fallen prey to the spiritualizing or marginalizing of Christian faith—have too often placed such hope in America. Thereby, the church has served as a sort of patronizing chaplain, a sort of court prophet dispensing spirituality while America goes on its way doing what it does without regard to the claims of the authority of Christ. Or the church has prostituted itself, dispensing its favors in exchange for a bit of influence in intimate chambers of power.

For Christians to extricate themselves from this theological captivity—often of Christians' own making—it must be stated clearly: the United States is not the hope of the world. The United States is not a Christian nation and never has been. The United States cannot be either of these because it is not within the province of a nation to be either the hope of the world or Christian. It would be like asserting that "this water is dry" or "the sunshine is dark."

Consequently, to place any ultimate hope in the nation-state is foolish. The historical records clearly demonstrate that all empires have fallen. On historical grounds, and certainly on biblical grounds, we may safely presume that all empires will. Because such a bastardized hope in any empire or nation-state is foolish, the deep partisan hostilities that pervade contemporary Christianity are a further perversion of Christian faith. The ideologically committed Christian Republican who can see no good in the Democrat or Green Party has denied the faith. The ideologically committed Christian Democrat who can see no good in the Republican or Tea Party has denied the faith.

To move beyond such an ideologically narrow vision requires forsaking simplistic or selective readings of the Bible. We must stop redacting Scripture. So-called Christian values corrupt Christianity. Instead, a rightfully informed Christian politic must be adept with a thick accounting of the Christian tradition. Such a reading of the biblical text and the great tradition of the church will provide a host of riches with which to address contemporary concerns.

This being committed most seriously to the Christian tradition does not mean that the principalities and powers are irrelevant, insignificant, or to be ignored. The New Testament assumes a certain fallenness of the powers that be. Yet it also assumes a created goodness to such powers, located in their purpose to serve humankind. Consequently, Christianity rightfully has a great deal of interest in the relative political goods that the powers may engender or inhibit.

But in relating to the powers that be, Christianity must first understand itself well. Christianity must insist that it is not a religion, a sort of privatized set of convictions regarding the afterlife. Instead, Christianity is an alternative politic. It is precisely the content of this alternative politic that makes it impossible for any nation-state to be Christian. And it is precisely the content of this alternative politic that makes it impossible for Christianity to run the world. Liberal political puissance will not restore the witness of Christianity in America but only further deepen its failure. Instead, the alternative politic—of witnessing, sharing, forgiving, reconciling, extending hospitality—entails exhibiting to the world what the world was intended to be.

This summarizes the argument to this point.

Such a depiction of Christian faith has been wrongly summarized as a stance of *withdrawal*. Others have dubbed such a stance as *sectarian*. These two false assessments must be addressed and then an alternate construal proposed.

Withdrawal from Culture Is Simply Not an Option

Withdrawal is a literal impossibility. Anyone who suggests that we should withdraw from culture exhibits a fundamental ignorance about terms. *Culture* is not something from which one can simply withdraw. Culture comprises language, music, art, and numerous other forms of social communication, engagement, and character development. One cannot withdraw from such and still be human in any meaningful sense. To make such a claim makes as much sense as telling a fish to withdraw from water or humans to withdraw from air. Culture is the air we breathe, in which human communities subsist, exist, coexist. We simply cannot withdraw from culture, because culture is what makes us human, at least humans who are in any sense rightly understood as social beings.[1]

Similarly, Christians must banish the ignorant but generally well-intentioned talk of being countercultural. Such claims confuse more than they clarify. In being countercultural, are we to be opposed to speaking English? To Americana music? To banjos or electric guitars or iPads? To William Faulkner or Max Lucado or Johnny Cash? This pious call to be countercultural, unless carefully qualified, may foster condescension or an unnecessary disdainful hostility. Or in some cases this call to be countercultural correlates with a pious anti-intellectualism.

All of these tendencies stand at odds with our desired political witness.

On the Charge of Sectarianism

The word *sectarian* is commonly employed to mean excessively devoted to a partisan view or narrow set of commitments. Of-

---

1. H. Richard Niebuhr's *Christ and Culture* did a great disservice to the last century of American theological reflection. By envisioning culture as a homogenous, autonomous entity, Niebuhr posits it as an authority over against Christ that one must accept, reject, or synthesize. Niebuhr then types those who uncompromisingly adhere to the authority of Christ as radicals who withdraw from social or political involvement. But as I argue here, culture is more accurately portrayed as the field of human activity that the Christian community selectively engages, seeking to transform human history and societies through adherence to the lordship of Christ.

ten the term connotes an unwillingness to give credence to truth claims or authorities beyond those of the sect itself. In popular usage *sectarian* may further connote the tendency of a group to discount or demean or at worst seek to destroy the dignity or humanity of those outside the sect.

Three subpoints are in order:

1. If by the charge of *sectarianism* one simply means that a Christian is first and foremost devoted to the authority of Christ, then let us hope such an accusation will stand. There is a certain legitimate sectarianism of Christianity that we would do well to pursue, that is, to have a clear sense of the manner in which the politic of Christianity provides a constructive alternative to, and stands at odds with, some significant elements of American capitalism or Russian socialism or North Korean militarism or Hollywood sentimentalism or Fifth Avenue commodificationism.

(It is possible that many who use the term *countercultural* are wanting in fact to say something like this, in which case they would be quite correct. But to use the term *countercultural* misconstrues the situation and creates unnecessary hostility, judgment, or antipathy.)

Again, if the charge of sectarianism is simply that we Christians are upholding the teachings and authority of Christ above all other authorities, then we need not fear. But this is not typically the problem with Christianity in America.

2. The charge of sectarianism may mean something much less admirable. It may entail the sort of critique leveled at either ISIS radicals or Christian theocrats calling for a return to a supposed Christian America. This is a sort of sectarianism unworthy, for reasons we have already seen, of those who would be Christians.

The charge of sectarianism, similarly, could entail a sort of standoffishness, a sort of judgmental piety that refuses to engage its neighbors, refuses to seek the good of the city, or refuses to partner with those who do not share a claim to the lordship of Christ; or worse, refuses to partner with those who do not share all the jots and tittles of particular denominational commitments. The biblical vision, in contrast, offers a lavish vision of human possibility grounded in its generous vision, promiscuous even, of the love of God. Moreover, the biblical insistence that the principalities and powers have been overcome in the truth telling and suffering love of Christ and that the Spirit and resurrecting power of God have been unleashed in new ways in human history—these realities open up space for unimaginable possibilities to arise in the midst of our communities.

All these basic biblical commitments, and many more, should make it clear that Christianity, rightly understood, overwhelms this sort of sectarianism. If "captivity has been taken captive," then our basic posture, in which we are different only for the sake of the glory of God and for sake of the good of the nations, can only be one fundamentally at odds with sectarianism itself. In other words, our so-called sectarianism requires us to celebrate whatever common graces and common pursuits and common goodwill we may find and wherever we may find them. Our divergent morality is one that requires us not to withdraw but always be in a missional mode, engaging, celebrating, challenging, seeking the good of the city. The Old Testament vision of Israel and the New Testament vision of the church both depict distinctive communities always in service to the nations and never in opposition to them for the sake of opposition. Israel and the church, in the biblical tradition, are different not for the sake of being different, not for the sake of condemnation, but for the sake of service and witness to the true goods of human history.

3. While we are right to critique these sorts of sectarian tendencies in Christianity, *let us not overlook the sectarianism of the nation-state.* Let us not fail to note that when French Christians were arrayed against German Christians in World War I, they were not fighting for competing visions of sectarian Christianity but for the sectarian nation-state in which they had been born. When the United States napalms Vietnamese villagers, when Japan rapes China, when Stalin slaughters millions of his own, or when Germany gasses millions of Jews, it is clear that the great sectarianism of the late-modern world is not the religious debates between the Baptists and the Methodists or even the narrow-

minded Christians all aflutter about posting the Ten Commandments in the state house. No, at least when it comes to matters
of life and death, the great sectarianism of our day is that of the
industrialized killing done in allegiance to and in the self-interest
of the nation-state.

Percipient Cultural Discernment and Cultural Production

Our task, then, is no ill-conceived insistence that we Christians
should be countercultural. (Such a posture would be akin to someone sharply opposed to profanity insisting we must be opposed to
language, that we must be counterlanguage.) Instead, we are called
to a percipient cultural discernment: a deep capacity to rightly
understand cultural phenomena in many facets and multiple implications and, with such understanding, discern a path forward
that bears witness to the good news of the kingdom of God in our
midst.

Our task, in other words, is *not* to see ourselves as H. Richard Niebuhr would have it, as a people with an abstract faith that
must somehow be set in relation to a monistic culture, choosing
an overall strategy to withdraw, accommodate, or transform that
culture. No, quite to the contrary. We rightfully understand ourselves as people of faith swimming in the water of whatever culture
in which we find ourselves. There in the cultural water will be a
great variety of particular realities floating about. Some of these
we will celebrate, some we will reject, some we will want to see
transformed into a redemptive human practice. But there will be
no celebrating, withdrawing from, or transforming the water of
culture as a whole.

From some cultural practices we *maintain an insistent withdrawal.* For instance, the objectification of women and children in
prostitution, the salacious use of sex to arouse consumerist desires,
or the systematic manner in which we are taught to hate and then
systematically kill our enemies while feeling patriotically noble
about it.

Some exemplary Christian achievements in this area have included the civil rights movement, arising out of the black church in America, in which an explicit commitment to Christian nonviolence was conjoined with an explicit commitment to withdraw from particular structures and systems of oppression. Because of a refusal to participate any longer in unjust business practices, the self-interest of the local economic powers that be led to reform. The abolitionist movement provides another example, in the likes of the devoted Christian William Wilberforce, who committed his life to the withdrawal of English legal protections of and participation in slavery.

In some cultural practices we *wholeheartedly engage*: voluntary sharing of wealth and resources and seeking best practices for the holistic flourishing of communities, practices of forgiveness and reconciliation, the practices of music and art and poetry, which facilitate the liberation of the human spirit and the joy of living. Victim-offender reconciliation programs, symphonies, and art galleries; Marilynne Robinson and Andrew Peterson and Chris Wiman and Wendell Berry and Tracy K. Smith; Habitat for Humanity and rightly configured bankruptcy laws; low-interest mortgages for the poor and community development that attends not just to the wealthy but to those potentially marginalized by gentrification or other forms of wealth accumulation.

In yet other cultural practices we will seek a *redemptive transformation*, engaging with care, celebrating some particulars and critiquing yet others: celebrating a free press, for example, as an institution that at its best seeks to preserve the possibility of public truth-telling as a means of inhibiting oppression, and yet critiquing the manner in which capitalist concerns may undercut and subvert the truth-telling goals of that very institution. Or celebrating a free-and-fair exchange of goods as a mechanism for facilitating the economic well-being of a community and yet critiquing the manner in which the lust for power is often at play in the disciplines of marketing and the rise of the transnational corporation.

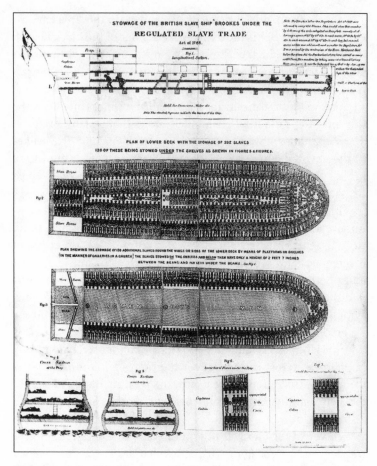

Stowage of the British slave ship *Brookes* under the regulated slave trade act of 1788, December 1788. *Library of Congress Rare Book and Special Collections. Wikimedia Commons*

Beyond practices of discernment regarding existing cultural artifacts, we will *do our own culture making*: let us not forget that grand institutional and cultural contributions like the hospital and the university were propagated and facilitated by the Christian tradition, nor can we overlook the contributions made in many fields due to and arising out of Christian practice in Newtonian physics, architecture, Mendelian genetics, and much more besides.

Of course, these examples are painted in broad strokes but are nonetheless illustrative of a constructive way forward. And these examples set the stage for the final commitment of our political manifesto: that Christian social engagement must always be *ad hoc*.

Christian Engagement
Must Always Be *Ad Hoc*

SUMMARY

Christian social engagement must always be *ad hoc*. Given that we live between the time of the inauguration and the consummation of the kingdom of God, there is no ideologically pure or utopian social arrangement among the nations for which we should strive. Any given social structure—no matter its strengths—is prone to fall under the sway of the powers of sin. Once one injustice is corrected with some new practice of equity, the new practice will, in turn, struggle with its own infidelities with regard to greed or pride or coercive force. Then a new corrective must be sought, and then again yet another.

To continue ever to seek such new correctives—gracious and fair and equitable social practices—with patience and peaceableness and truth telling and without coercion or violence or disdain, this is what it means to be living as a Christian, as a Christian community, in the world prior to the consummation of the kingdom of God.

EXPOSITION

Dietrich Bonhoeffer claimed that

> Jesus concerns himself hardly at all with the solution of worldly problems. When He is asked to do so His answer is remarkably

evasive. . . . Indeed, He scarcely ever replies to men's questions
directly, but answers rather from a quite different plane. His
word is not an answer to human questions and problems; it is
the answer of God to the question of God to man. His word is
essentially determined not from below but from above. It is not
a solution, but a redemption.[1]

But neither did Jesus concern himself with a solution to the problem of cancer, questions about evolutionary theory, responses to
environmental degradation, or the grave threat of annihilation by
nuclear weapons. Nonetheless, Bonhoeffer rightly reminds us by
his words quoted here that Jesus announced the coming of the
kingdom of God and inaugurated its presence, and that this reality
is indeed a redemption and not a mere solution to human problems. And Bonhoeffer is quite right to insist that the "word," which
is a "redemption," is indeed what "must first of all be understood.
Instead of the solution to problems, Jesus brings the redemption"
of humankind, and then "for that very reason He does really bring
the solution of all human problems as well."[2]

But: it does seem that we must take seriously what the so-
called realists have insisted, that we must take seriously that the
kingdom come has not yet come fully. In other words, we must
not forget that Jesus did not finish what he started—Jesus did not
consummate, has not yet consummated the fullness of the kingdom of God—and, so far as the Gospels relate, he left that day and
time and deed to the working of God.

We then are left between the times to bear witness through
creative solutions to complex problems and ever-shifting realities—ever shifting because of, among other things, the abiding
power of sin—from our own distinctive way of life, for the good
of the nations.

This simple observation, grounded in a New Testament escha-
tology, is profound and far-reaching in freeing us from ideological

1. Dietrich Bonhoeffer, *Ethics* (New York: Simon & Schuster, 1955), 350.
2. Bonhoeffer, *Ethics*, 350.

commitments to any given partisan solution to any given problem. If any given institution, party, or policy can (and does) yet fall prey to the power of sin, does yet fall prey to the power of death, then we are always allowed, even required, to do equal-opportunity critique of the institution of the church as much as the institutions of government or other social or economic institutions and structures, and look for ways in which some limited solution in that given context can bear witness to the gracious reign of God broken in but not yet consummated.

Consider the nonideological engagement with centralized governmental power in the biblical story. When the pharaoh has a dream, which the boy Joseph foretells is an omen of a coming great famine, the solution to the problem is a vast project of taxation and centralized bureaucracy. It is through such centralization that the Hebrews are saved, and such a development is celebrated in the telling of the biblical story. Let those ideologically opposed to big government and centralization take note and beware.

And yet, of course, the story does not end there. As the narrative unfolds, the very centralized bureaucracy that was one season a practical solution to a dire social need becomes in the next season the mechanism for enslavement and oppression. When a pharaoh arose "who did not know Joseph," then that mechanism became the means of the enslavement of the Hebrews it once saved. There is, indeed, a danger to such mechanisms of power, and the danger is put on display in the biblical story. Let those ideologically committed to big government and centralization take note and beware.

In the apostle Paul's teaching, he depicts the old covenant and the law as a mechanism through which sin can manifest its capacity for oppression. Imagine the freedom that such a realization gives the Christian church in America. If the law of God, given by Moses, can become an apparatus of death, how much more so can American jurisprudence? What then if we realize that the target will always be shifting, and to place too much hope in any given legislative agenda will be a dashed hope?

Take, for example, Michael Lewis's book *Flash Boys: A Wall Street Revolt*. There Lewis documents how well-intentioned and much-needed federal regulation gives rise to an entire financial subculture of high-frequency trading that games the system, taking advantage of that regulation, making billions of dollars out of its own greed. Indeed, Lewis suggests that this dynamic occurs repeatedly in the history of fiscal regulation in the United States. Today's crisis, emerging out of the dynamics of broken and self-serving impulses, gives rise to new regulation, which becomes the seedbed of the next round of greedily gaming the system.[3]

To use New Testament language, we might say then that greed—as a systemic corrupt impulse—is indeed subtle and powerful, and no financial regulation will ever be its consummate solution, will ever be its final redemption. Lewis simply illustrates with his indictment of twenty-first-century Wall Street what the apostle Paul knew long ago about the power of law.

Such an observation may allow us greater wisdom in bearing witness to the kingdom of God. We need not become single-issue voters, for example.[4] We need not assume one piece of legislation is the only way forward. Those with conservative liberal tendencies, for example, may be opened to appreciate what appears counterintuitive to them: that there is substantive evidence that rates of abortion go down significantly under Democratic presidential administrations in contrast to Republican administrations.[5] On the other hand, those with liberal liberal tendencies may be opened to appreciate that care for the poor may be broader than welfare mechanisms that fail to take the development of human virtue seriously.

---

3. Michael Lewis, *Flash Boys: A Wall Street Revolt* (New York: W. W. Norton, 2015).

4. Note my care in language. I am not suggesting there would never be a time or context in which being a single-issue voter would be out of bounds. I am suggesting instead that we need not presume that one piece of legislation might be the panacea we expect, after all, and thus other ways forward are made available to us.

5. See T. C. Jatlaoui et al., "Abortion Surveillance—United States," *Surveillance Summaries* 67, no. 13 (2018): 1–45, https://www.cdc.gov/mmwr/volumes/67/ss/ss6713a1.htm.

Evelyn de Morgan, *The Worship of Mammon*, ca. 1909, oil on canvas, De Morgan Centre, London. *Wikimedia Commons*

Such an eschatological realism—that the kingdom of God has come, but not yet come in full—need not drive us, as it has so often in Christian history, to set aside the way of Christ.

Does this insistence, though—that Christians seek to submit themselves to the way of Christ in all roles in which they find themselves—mean that Christians really have nothing to say to the powers that be who refuse to take up the way of Christ?

Certainly not.

First, this eschatological realism—in which we are constantly attending to the fact that the kingdom of God has come, but not yet fully, and thus (a) all our best attempts at bearing witness to the present-and-coming kingdom are always prone to and always tend toward sin, and (b) that all the best and varied social practices and political commitments are also struggling under the domination of sin and death—allows us to let go the unrealistic idealism or utopianism that drives partisan visions. It allows us to let go of our own nationalisms. This eschatological realism allows us to let ourselves see both the good and bad of any given party, any given nation-state. We must continue to insist that Christians are not utopian idealists. This is true precisely because our vision of history and life is informed by such eschatological realism. Christians who strive to live by the Sermon on the Mount (rightfully understood, of course) are not the idealists and utopians. It is the ideologues, the partisans, the nationalists who are the dangerous utopians. It is this utopianism that sows the seeds of hostility and reaps a warring madness.

No social structure—including the church and the members of the church—will transcend the detritus of death prior to the consummation of the kingdom of God. This position is not pessimism. It is grounded in an eschatological hope, a hope already breaking into our midst. Nor is this position cynical, because it is not interested in judging others. It is interested in making concrete and specific contributions of service to the world that simultaneously take seriously the deep brokenness of all things.

Second, this approach then makes space for political realism: not in granting such political realism status as authoritative for ethics or policy or Christian life, but in its capacity to see things, to see power dynamics at play that we may not be able to see otherwise. Political realism stereotypically avoids utopian or idealistic visions of politics, with a deep awareness of the depths to which the human hankering after power stoops. Its solution—of a moderated self-interest, always balancing power with counterpower—cannot well serve Christian ethics because it replaces the normativity of Christ with the normativity of the self-interest of nation-states, rulers, or some select group to the exclusion of others. But its insight regarding power dynamics may serve us. First, in being an ally with Christians to critique the nationalists and utopians; and second, in helping Christians understand the deep working of power and self-interest in the world.

We must make clear our insistence on taking seriously the way of Christ—even granting that we are always falling short, always needing to repent again—our insistence on upholding the way of Christ as our norm for our lives. But as seen, this does not mean we have nothing to share with the unbelieving social orders that cannot or will not accept Christ as Lord. This can be true if and only if the social practices of the gospel are indeed in line with the grain of the universe, only if the social practices of reconciliation and sharing and truth telling and forgiveness are in fact consistent with the fundamental nature of being human.

We do believe and proclaim that they are. Consequently, there is a great and broad playing field in which we may make contributions. We can seek solutions to concrete human problems, whether medicinal or social or political or economic, and offer these as good news to our communities. We may do social science research to find constructive ways to deal with the opioid epidemic that are superior, more effective, and less costly than those of the criminal justice system, and help liberal liberals and conservative liberals alike see how such solutions may satisfy both their deepest concerns. We may contribute from our studies in nonviolence such means that may be used in community policing to minimize the use of force, especially lethal force, and thus the hostility that is threatening many of our communities. We may pursue neurological research that promises new possibilities in understanding the cultivation of various social virtues such as compassion, self-control, and empathy, which may make possible holding together tenuous and fragile bonds of community. We may seek to map the human genome and beat the capitalists to their own mapping so that such knowledge might be in the public domain and thus accessible to a broader swath of humankind.[6]

And we may, on the side of critique, call rulers, even tyrants and despots, to change and take steps in the direction of the kingdom of God. That is, even if they refuse to acknowledge the authority of Christ, we may still bear witness to the beauty of truth or goodness and call them to take such seriously. For example, the tyrant can be called to repent of his lying and self-aggrandizement and violence, especially to the degree that these poison the community. For some, the step away from lying and into truth telling will be as great as an unbeliever stepping into a confession of faith. We should not take lightly the potential consequences power brokers may face when we ask them to tell the truth or stop their violence or welcome the stranger.

As Christians we would have all people—statesmen, presidents, queens, and kings—submit to the way of Christ. This would be, undoubtedly, a dangerous proposition for a president or king or queen: to love one's enemies, to forgive debts, to refuse to do to them what they have done to us. All this would be highly dangerous for a leader of a nation-state. It may get him or her killed, and certainly could get him or her thrown or voted out of office. Such consequences, however, are the dangers of public leadership generally considered. One may get thrown out of office, not voted back into office, or assassinated for many other reasons than seeking to submit to the way of Christ while in office.

But even if they will not or cannot take up the lordship of Christ, there will remain many constructive steps toward the liberating ways of the kingdom of God. And it is those next steps, those next dangerous, risky steps toward such liberation, to which we seek, winsomely, to call the as-yet-unbelieving ruler.

6. I heard Francis Collins, who led the Human Genome Project, recount that this was one of the driving forces behind his own (Christian) commitment to helping map the human genome as a part of the publicly funded pursuit he was a part of.

Such an approach grants us immense liberty—liberty, we might hopefully note, much greater than the bondage of party affiliation apparently affords Washington politicians. In strategic fashion—"be wise as serpents and innocent as doves"—we can, and should, look for places of common cause, of moves in the right direction, and celebrate and facilitate such moves.[7]

Our own proleptic living—trusting that the magnificent Spirit of God makes possible impossible possibilities, even now—allows us to go forth and sow the seeds of the kingdom of God, knowing that history is not one damn meaningless thing after another but the stage for the brilliant inbreaking of the final hope of God. It will not be the hope of America; it will not be the hope of any nation-state. It will be the hope of the Christ who breaks down all walls of hostility, making all things new, for captivity has, after all, been taken captive and death already undone.

7. At the same time, our theologically prioritized social critiques may provide helpful and needed correctives to the political philosophers who often begin with what they believe can be commonly known.

Afterword

In days to come
    the mountain of the LORD's house
shall be established as the highest of the mountains,
    and shall be raised above the hills;
all the nations shall stream to it.
    Many peoples shall come and say,
"Come, let us go up to the mountain of the LORD,
    to the house of the God of Jacob;
that he may teach us his ways
    and that we may walk in his paths."
For out of Zion shall go forth instruction,
    and the word of the LORD from Jerusalem.
He shall judge between the nations,
    and shall arbitrate for many peoples;
they shall beat their swords into plowshares,
    and their spears into pruning hooks;
nation shall not lift up sword against nation,
    neither shall they learn war any more.   (Isa. 2:2–4)

The good news proffered by Jesus of Nazareth claims that the coming kingdom has come: not yet fully but it *has* come, it has begun. The fundamental political question of our day is not, cannot be, then, a partisan one. The fundamental political question of our day is whether we who would be Christians will live in such a way as to exemplify the kingdom come and the kingdom coming.

Dag Hammarskjöld, one of the highest-profile secretary-generals of the United Nations in the twentieth century, apparently thought of himself something like an anonymous Christian. He lived a storied life, one of privilege, which he sought to yield to the purposes of God, consciously giving his career as well as his life to do God's will as best he understood it. At the end of a courageous career, his plane went down on a peacemaking mission in Africa. It is thought by some that he was assassinated.

After his death an unpublished manuscript was found in his personal effects: a collection of parables, aphorisms, and observations about life, meditations on the meaning of his life vis-à-vis the story of the gospel. Published posthumously, *Markings* preserves the wisdom of a man who thought a great deal, not merely about his character defects but also about the possibilities of living a life of authentic freedom and maturity. He knew that this ultimate freedom, in light of the gospel, entailed the freedom to die.

This sort of freedom, Hammarskjöld well understood, is not merely a sort of grit-your-teeth, white-knuckled willingness to be assassinated. After all, deep self-centeredness may pervert self-sacrifice into self-absorbed heroism. "The 'great' commitment is so much easier than the ordinary everyday one—and can all too easily shut our hearts to the latter. A willingness to make the ultimate sacrifice can be associated with, and even produce, a great hardness of heart."[1]

Hammarskjöld was after something quite different, a sort of freedom that yields oneself to God's purposes, a freedom to endure the long and challenging chapters of human maturation, facing one's pettiness and ambition and greed for power and fear for one's legacy, all of which may destroy the "great commitment" of giving one's all. He exemplifies a man grappling with power and possibility and politics and struggling after a maturity that surrenders control. "Maturity: among other things, a new lack of self-consciousness—the kind

---

1. Dag Hammarskjöld, *Markings*, trans. Leif Sjöberg and W. H. Auden (New York: Alfred A. Knopf, 1964), 131.

you can only attain when you have become entirely indifferent to yourself through an absolute assent to your fate. He who has placed himself in God's hand stands free vis-à-vis men: he is entirely at his ease with them, because he has granted them the right to judge."[2] His politics and peacemaking was never the sort that was a passive indulgence of others. "It is easy to be nice, even to an enemy—from lack of character." "Never, 'for the sake of peace and quiet,' deny your own experience or convictions." And yet the great commitment required, obviously, a tender love.

The "great" commitment all too easily obscures the "little" one. But without the humility and warmth which you have to develop in your relations to the few with whom you are personally involved, you will never be able to do anything for the many. Without them, you will live in a world of abstractions, where your solipsism, your greed for power, and your death-wish lack the one opponent which is stronger than they—love. Love, which is without an object, the outflowing of a power released by self-surrender, but which would remain a sublime sort of superhuman self-assertion, powerless against the negative forces within you, if it were not tamed by the yoke of human intimacy and warmed by its tenderness.[3]

When Hammarskjöld commissioned a meditation room to be built in the United Nations headquarters in New York, he—along with Christians, Jews, and Muslims—decided that no traditional symbols would be employed in that space. Instead, a six-and-one-half-ton block of iron ore was placed in the center of the small room, a fixture above projecting a shaft of light onto the rectangular block. In his commentary, Hammarskjöld says, "The material of the stone leads our thoughts to the necessity for choice between destruction and construction, between war and peace. Of iron man has forged his swords, of iron he has also made his plowshares.

2. Hammarskjöld, *Markings*, 90.
3. Hammarskjöld, *Markings*, 133.

Of iron he has constructed tanks, but of iron he has likewise built homes for man. The block of iron ore is part of the wealth we have inherited on this earth of ours. How are we to use it?"[4]

Will our lives be governed by a vision of employing the bounty of the creation—its iron and its ores, its land and its crops—to care for the tender social fabric, to engender the goods of human flourishing? We who have been set free—in a deep and thick and multifaceted freedom, even unto death—are thus set free to employ the wealth at our disposal, not merely in terms of financial capital but wealth in all its manifold forms, in a manner that befits the coming kingdom of God. This is one of the great questions posed by the gospel: shall our brilliance and talents, our wealth and our means, be employed in service to the hostilities of the old aeon and the ways of captivity? Or to the inbreaking of the new and its ways of setting captives free, demolishing strongholds, and defeating all the handmaidens of death?

In an ironic inversion of the gospel, there is a tragic admission on a historical marker in Nashville on Eighth Avenue South. It reads:

NASHVILLE PLOW WORKS

Site of a farm implement factory operated by Messrs. Sharp and Hamilton, previous to the War Between the States. With the outbreak of hostilities they reversed the Biblical injunction and produced swords of excellent quality for the Confederacy. With the coming of the Federal Army, the making of swords was discontinued.

Thus stands the parable of the scandalous reversal of the biblical vision of peace: that sectarian loyalties and partisan commitments lead not merely to ignoring the call of the gospel but inverting them, perverting them. Beating our plows into swords, our hearts and politics formed not by the crucifixion and resurrection

4. Dag Hammarskjöld, "'A Room of Quiet,' The Meditation Room, United Nations Headquarters," *UN.org*, accessed July 19, 2019, http://www.un.org/depts /dhl/dag/meditationroom.htm.

Site of the Nashville Plow Works, Historical Commission of Metropolitan Nashville, 1967.

of the Messiah, we pant after the coming of another strongman bearing bigger and better swords, our hope bastardized by illicit intimacies, profaned and mocked.

May we become a new sort of scandal in the world, marked by the courage made possible by cross and resurrection, going forth with our faces toward the Son, sowing the seeds of the peaceable reign of God, come now and coming.

Amen.

Index

Note: Page numbers in italics denote illustrative material.

For More Resources

Please visit:

> www.LeeCCamp.com/scandalous
> www.TokensShow.com

Or follow on social media at:

> www.Facebook.com/leeccamp
> www.Instagram.com/leeccamp